KW-223-031

HISTORY VINDICATED

IN THE CASE OF

THE WIGTOWN MARTYRS.

BY THE

REV. ARCHIBALD STEWART,

MINISTER OF GLASSERTON

SECOND EDITION.

EDINBURGH:

EDMONSTON AND DOUGLAS.

1869.

In the interest of creating a more extensive selection of rare historical book reprints, we have chosen to reproduce this title even though it may possibly have occasional imperfections such as missing and blurred pages, missing text, poor pictures, markings, dark backgrounds and other reproduction issues beyond our control. Because this work is culturally important, we have made it available as a part of our commitment to protecting, preserving and promoting the world's literature. Thank you for your understanding.

HERE LYES MARGRAT
WILLSON DOUGHTER
TO GILBERT WILLSON
IN GLENVERNOCH·
WHO WAS DROUNED
ANNO 1685 AGED 18·

LET EARTH AND STONE STILL WITNES BEARE
HEIR LYES A VIRGINE MARTYRE HERE
MURTHER'D FOR OUNING CHRIST SUPREAME
HEAD OF HIS CHURCH AND NO MORE CRIME
BUT NOT ABJURING PRESBYTRY,
AND HER NOT OUNING PRELACY,
THEY HER CONDEM'D, BY UNJUST LAW,
OF HEAVEN NOR HELL THEY STOOD NO AW
WITHIN THE SEA TY'D TO A STAKE
SHE SUFFERED FOR CHRIST JESUS SAKE
THE ACTORS OF THIS CRUEL CRIME
WAS LAGG·STRACHAN·WINRAM·AND GRHAME
NEITHER YOUNG YEARES NOR YET OLD AGE
COULD STOP THE FURY OF THEIR RAGE·

FACSIMILE FROM PHOTOGRAPH OF MARGARET WILSON'S TOMBSTONE
IN WIGTOWN CHURCH YARD.

7

PREFACE TO THE SECOND EDITION.

———

THOUGH this little book met with a very favourable reception on its first appearance, that is not the reason why a *Second Edition* is now offered to the Public. So many *new* proofs (some of which have been published in an ephemeral shape) have come to light, that it is thought desirable to collect the whole in a permanent form. This task the Author has undertaken, at the suggestion of those to whose opinion he could not but pay deference. If he has succeeded in collecting and exhibiting such evidence as shall settle the controversy on the question at issue, and at the same time vindicate Wodrow's credibility as a *narrator of facts*, he shall have no occasion to regret the trouble (not inconsiderable) which he has had in doing so. The greater part of the Pamphlet has been re-written, so it may be considered rather a new work than a new edition. The Author is glad to take the opportunity of expressing thanks to those who have kindly aided him by lending him documents, rare books, and pamphlets. To one friend he owes special thanks—the Rev. Thomas Gordon, of Newbattle, who has, with much trouble, made investigations in the Register House, Edinburgh, and in the public libraries, which the Author, from remoteness, could not easily have done.

GLASSERTON MANSE,
February 1869.

INTRODUCTION.

T HE following pages are designed to exhibit the proof of a historical fact which has lately been disputed, viz. the execution, by
drowning, of Margaret Lauchlison and Margaret Wilson, at Wigtown,
during the persecution for religion in 1685. This fact was stated in the
controversial pamphlets of the time, and was never *directly* denied. A
full account of it was published in Wodrow's *History* in 1722, on the
authority of the local church courts, who made themselves responsible
for its truth. Though this story of martyrdom was thus officially
given to the world just thirty-seven years after the event is said to
have taken place, and while many were still living who were personally
acquainted with all the facts of the case, no one came forward *then* to
say, 'This story is false and calumnious.' In place of being contradicted and disproved, it has been repeated as a fact by all respectable
historians down to our times. It is only lately that it has been called
in question by Mr. Napier, in his *Memorials of Dundee*, and in his
more recent work, the *Case for the Crown*, expressly designed to prove
the Wigtown martyrs 'to be myths,' and the received story regarding
them to be a 'fable' and a 'calumny.'

Every one who values history has reason anxiously to inquire if
Mr. Napier has really succeeded in proving the negative in this case,
because, if he has, his argument will extend much farther than merely
to the case of the Wigtown women, which in itself, he says, 'would
be a trifling question to deal with elaborately and systematically.'
His design is to show that the history of Scotland during the Restoration period has been falsely written;—not merely that a wrong inter-
pretation has been put upon the events of the period, and false lessons
deduced from them, but that the events themselves have been falsely
set down;—that what Wodrow has given for history 'is a calumnious
tissue of monstrous fables.' The motto of the *Case for the Crown* is,
'*ex uno disce omnes*'—the Wigtown story is false; so are all the others.
'Weeded of fable, calumny, and fanatical railing,' says Mr. Napier,
'Wodrow's two folio volumes would vanish, or resolve into an appendix
of public documents that contradict him.'[1]

Mr. Napier's avowed design, then, is to destroy the credibility of

[1] *Case for the Crown*—Preface.

Wodrow, who, he informs us, 'has misled all our historians of mark, from David Hume to Lord Macaulay, who have blindly followed him, and lazily or lovingly submitted to his rubbish without an attempt at investigation. And thus it is,' he continues, 'that the national character of Scotland has been defamed by a mock and mythical martyrology of the lowest stamp, and her soil desecrated by fanatical monuments, not to commemorate martyrs, but to perpetuate a calumny.'[1] It is well that he admits, that in the 'weeding' which he thinks Wodrow needs, the 'public documents' quoted—the Acts of the Scotch Parliament, the Royal Letters and Proclamations, the Records of the Privy Council, and of the Courts of Justice—are still to be left, when all the fables and other rubbish are to be cleared away. If the public documents of the Restoration period are left as authentic materials of its history, it will give Mr. Napier some trouble to get quit of the martyrology, and to persuade intelligent and unpre-judiced minds, that the monuments of those who suffered in those times are to be looked on now, not as commemorating martyrs, but as perpetuating a calumny. Wodrow made large use of public documents. These, he tells us in his preface, 'are the great fund of which this history is formed.' As he proceeds year by year through the dreary period of the Restoration, he not only analyzes and com-ments on these documents, but quotes them at large; and he thus puts it in his reader's power to judge for himself, and to differ in opinion if he see cause. He says: 'I design that as little of this history as may be should lean upon me; let every one see with his own eyes and judge for himself, upon the very same evidence I have.'

But a history made up of Acts of Parliament and Council, and of Records of Justiciary, would be a very dull one; Wodrow, therefore, collected materials from other sources. He was himself the first who attempted a *history* of the Church of Scotland during the Restoration, though others had written *memoirs* of it in different shapes. These he had before him, and doubtless also the controversial pamphlets which were written both before and after the Revolution. But next to public documents, Wodrow was doubtless most indebted for the materials of his history to the accounts of the sufferings for religion within their bounds, furnished to him by the several judicatories of the Church of Scotland. He was avowedly the historian of the Church of Scotland, and she gave him her countenance and aid in the execution of his work.

It is the statements of Wodrow, made on the authority of the Courts of the Church of Scotland, that Mr. Napier assails. He fixes on the account of the *Wigtown Martyrdom* as the point of attack, and to its demolition he devotes 142 pages of energetic pleading in his *Case for the Crown*. In his preface, having taken credit to himself for other good services done to the cause of Scottish history, he says: 'I now sit down before this last stronghold of the Wodrow martyro-

[1] *Case for the Crown*—Preface.

logy, and hope to leave it also in ruins.'[1] If this stronghold shall fall, as Mr. Napier so confidently expects, it is evident enough that Wodrow's credit as a historian must sustain irreparable damage,—the issuing of a calumny of a gross kind will have been proved against the Church of Scotland, and the future historian of the Restoration period must discredit the narratives of sufferings furnished by the church courts, or at least say that they rest on doubtful authority.

This is the grand result which Mr. Napier expects to follow from his labours in the field of Scottish history. But his efforts, so far as successful, would tend to further results, which we are sure he neither contemplates nor intends, viz. *to serve the cause of scepticism.* One of his converts might say to him, 'You have proved the Wigtown martyrs to be myths. What for 150 years has been looked on as a page of true history, and told as such by writers of every party, you have shown to be a "fable." This is all the more wonderful, as the thing said to be done—a public execution of a novel kind—must have attracted much attention and occasioned much talk, if it took place; and every one living in that part of the country must have heard of it. Without taking into account the statements of various pamphlets, the ministers and elders of the district who, twenty-six years after, certified it as a fact, could not but have known all about it; and though they had strong prejudices, they were apparently as good authorities as one usually gets in such matters of history. Besides, they gave their statements for immediate publication, and under the wholesome fear of contradiction; and when it was made public, it was never directly contradicted, and never attempted to be disproved till now. After this, what facts of history can one be very sure of? Even the gospels themselves may be most part fable.'[2]

But we are far from imputing to Mr. Napier any design to serve the cause of general scepticism in matters of history, especially of sacred history. We regard his object to be merely that which he plainly avows,—to cast discredit on the martyrology of Wodrow, and to prove against the ministers and elders of the Church of Scotland, in 1711, a charge of giving a false version of the history of their church, for the purpose of calumniating those who had for a time ruled this country in the interests and under the inspiration of Prelacy. His design is plainly avowed. Let ours be equally so. *It is*

---

[1] The first edition of *History Vindicated* was published in July 1867. Immediately thereafter Mr. Napier advertised a new edition of his *Case*, which has not appeared up to this date (February 1869). Is he still sitting before the stronghold? or has he raised the siege?

[2] Archbishop Whately, in the preface to the last edition of *Historical Doubts relative to Napoleon Bonaparte* (a satire on the scepticism of Hume), tells us that some of his 'sensible readers' complained of the difficulty of determining *what* they are to believe; and that he had 'been solicited to endeavour to frame some canons which may furnish a standard for determining what evidence is to be received.' Some of Mr. Napier's sensible readers may have come to him in similar difficulty.

to defend Wodrow and the Church of Scotland from Mr. Napier's attack —to prove that to be a fact which Mr. Napier imagines he has proved to be a myth—to prove the historical fact in question to be really true, and the authors of it to be no calumniators.

Let it be kept in mind that the matter in dispute is a matter of *fact*, and not of opinion. It is not any *opinions* which Wodrow may have expressed as to the events he records that we are now to defend, nor yet the 'spirit' he is thought to show, and the 'fanatical railing' in which he is said to have indulged. And we have as little intention of controverting Mr. Napier's opinions regarding the events of the period, or of inquiring if he has kept himself quite free from those vices of style which he blames in Wodrow. It may be the case that one who has been led 'to the conviction that not a single individual was unjustly put to death for rebellion or high treason in Scotland by the Governments of the Restoration,'[1] may have formed an opinion different from what is generally entertained; but it would certainly be premature to controvert this opinion, while the facts on which it must rest are still in dispute. The *facts* of history form the common ground on which men of all opinions must stand; and consequently all are alike interested in having them settled and fixed beyond dispute.

While our main design is to vindicate the history of Wodrow *as a statement of facts*, by establishing the truth of the case which has been singled out to be disproved, we have this further object in view,—*to preserve to the two sufferers the honour which has hitherto been paid to their memory*. If their singular history be true, their memory should not be allowed to perish. It may be said: These women were no martyrs, even if they did suffer death. *Non pœna, sed causa, facit martyrem :* Not the suffering, but the cause, makes the martyr. A martyr is one who dies for the truth. But did these women die for the truth, or any part of the truth, in suffering for Presbytery as opposed to Prelacy ? If their case be looked into, it will be seen that they suffered, not for adherence to any mere form of worship or church polity, but for something infinitely higher. They stood firmly to hear sentence of death passed on them, rather than take an oath which they believed it would be sinful in them to take. And (if the story be true) when reprieved, and offered the opportunity of escaping the death to which they had been doomed if they would take the oath, they refused to live on such terms. Even after they had tasted the bitterness of death, they refused life if it were to be purchased by doing what they believed to be sin. *They would rather die than sin against God.* That was their religion, and it was for that they suffered. Was not that true religion, and were not they sufferers for the truth, —martyrs, in the proper sense of the term ? To die rather than sin is the sublimest height of religion, in comparison with which, adherence to Presbytery or Episcopacy is a very small matter.

Some may think the oath that was offered to them a very simple

[1] *Case for the Crown*—Preface.

one, which any one peaceably disposed might have taken. *They* did not think so, and that was enough. They thought it would be morally wrong to swear that oath; and since they thought so, it would have been sin in them to take it. To swear a solemn oath is not quite so simple a thing as to eat flesh; yet there is the highest authority for believing, that he who even doubteth the lawfulness of the act, is condemned if he eat. Thus it is clear, that an act may be lawful and right in itself, and yet be sin in him whose conscience does not allow it. These simple countrywomen feared to sin against God by taking an oath which perhaps they did not very well understand, and which, at all events, their consciences did not allow them to take. They would, therefore, rather die than take that oath. If their story be true, theirs was indeed a martyrdom as worthy of a place on the page of history as many others recorded.

Mr. Napier's theory as to the Wigtown martyrdom has already received attention, and several able articles have been written in refutation of it. But the proof on the *affirmative* side of the question has not hitherto been fully stated. The following pages are intended to supply that defect. The church records of the period, and other local sources of evidence, have been examined, and many new facts bearing on the subject will be adduced.

If any think that Mr. Napier's argument does not call for an elaborate reply—that it is not likely to make many converts, we need only say, that it did for a time make converts even in Galloway, and more, doubtless, elsewhere, where the circumstances of the case are less known. Mr. Napier, in his preface to the *Case for the Crown*, is able to boast as the result of his argument, as stated in his *Memorials of Dundee*, that 'a leading English journal of letters' has pronounced, that though the Wigtown martyrdom may not be absolutely disproved, the proofs have been 'rudely shaken.' The *Case* may have completed, in the view of not a few, the work of demolition which the *Memorials* commenced. At all events, it is clear enough, that if no one will now take the trouble to collect and state the proofs of the martyrdom *while they can be collected*, the next generation will be more sceptical than the present, and the end of this will be, *a different version of history, very remote from truth, and very far from just towards the Church of Scotland.* No longer in the history of Scotland will be found a place for

> ' The life and death of martyrs, who sustained
> With will inflexible those fearful pangs,
> Triumphantly displayed in records left
> Of persecution and the Covenant,—times
> Whose echo rings through Scotland to this hour.'

CHAPTER I.

PREVIOUS LEGISLATION.

THOUGH it is not the object aimed at in these pages to vindicate the principles and proceedings of one party in the struggle which ended in the Revolution of 1688, and to cast blame upon the other, *but merely to establish a historical fact*, it is necessary to remind the reader of the leading events in the previous history, and to direct attention especially to the *legislation* of the period, so far as it relates to our subject. This is a necessary preliminary, especially as Mr. Napier endeavours, throughout his *Case for the Crown*, to make it appear that the imputation of *persecution* to the Restoration Governments is an invention of their enemies,— a calumny raised by Wodrow and the Church of Scotland. We shall let the reader judge of the Governments of the Restoration by *their own acts*, as these appear in public documents, which Wodrow quotes at length.[1]

When Charles II. was restored to the throne of his ancestors on 29th May 1660, he had no more loyal subjects than the Scottish Presbyterians; but few years had passed till wide discontent prevailed among them, and some were in rebellion. Who was to blame for this unhappy state of things? Let the reader look for the answer, not to anything Wodrow, or those who may have copied him, may have written, but to the Acts of the Scottish Parliament and Council, to which we shall endeavour to guide him.

Till a Parliament should be called in Scotland, the King committed the government to a Committee of Estates, who were authorized to meet on 23d August. On that same day ten ministers and elders met in a private house in Edinburgh (there being no meeting of the synods of the church till October) to draw up a humble address and supplication to the King regarding the church. The Committee of Estates, hearing of their meeting, seized their unfinished paper, and passed an Act for their imprisonment in the Castle.[2]

This first act of the King's Executive in Scotland looked rather

---

[1] Wodrow's *History* is invaluable, were it merely for the *public documents*, not otherwise easily accessible, which it contains. The reader will understand, when we refer to Wodrow, it is to direct attention to some of these, which he will find quoted at length. Our references are to Dr. Burns' edition, 4 vols. 8vo.

[2] Wodrow, vol. i. p. 71.

ominous; but a gracious letter from the King himself was fitted to quiet the fears of the less suspicious. This royal letter, dated 10th August 1660, was addressed to Mr. Robert Douglas, one of the ministers of Edinburgh, to be communicated to the Presbytery of Edinburgh, and made known throughout the church. It was delivered on the 1st September, having been brought from London by Mr. James Sharp, who had been sent thither by his brethren to promote the King's recall, and to look after the interests of the Presbyterian Church.[1] The King expressed himself well satisfied with the 'constant affection and loyalty' of the ministers of the church, and gave them this express assurance: ' *We do also resolve to protect and preserve the government of the Church of Scotland, as it is settled by law, without violation.*'[2] This assurance was of course understood in the natural sense of its terms, and called forth a most loyal and grateful answer.

Four months after (1st January 1661), the first Scottish Parliament of the restored King met at Edinburgh, the Earl of Middleton being his Majesty's Commissioner. A series of Acts were passed establishing the King's supremacy in all matters, civil and ecclesiastical, in unrestricted terms. The 15th Act of this notable Parliament, known as the 'Act Rescissory,' annulled all Parliaments and their proceedings since 1638; and thus at one sweep abolished all laws made in favour, not only of the Presbyterian Church, but of civil liberty. The next Act (16th), ' concerning religion and church government,' showed that the existing order of church government would not be long continued. ' As to the government of the church, his Majesty will make it his care to settle and secure the same in such a frame as shall be most agreeable to the word of God, most suitable to monarchical government, and most complying with the public peace and quiet of the kingdom. And, *in the meantime,* his Majesty, with advice and consent foresaid, doth allow the present administration by sessions, presbyteries, and synods (they keeping within bounds, and behaving themselves as said is), and that, notwithstanding of the preceding Act, rescissory of all pretended Parliaments since 1638.'[3]

When the Presbytery of Edinburgh, knowing that an Act had been passed withdrawing all the civil securities of their church, drew up a petition to Parliament reminding them of the terms of the King's letter addressed to them, their petition was not received.[4] And when in April the several synods had their ordinary meetings, and proceeded to consider the affairs of the church, and to avail themselves of their right of petitioning Parliament, their proceedings were interrupted by emissaries of the Government. A royal proclamation ' concerning church affairs,' dated 10th June, commends ' all

---

[1] How Mr. Sharp looked after the interests of the church and *his own*, may be inferred from the fact, that before the end of the following year he was the Primate of a Scottish episcopate.

[2] Wodrow, vol. i. p. 80.   [3] *Ibid.*, vol. i. p. 102.   [4] *Ibid.*, vol. i. p. 112.

our loving subjects, ministers, and others, as they will answer at their
peril, to abstain from meddling with what may concern the public
government of that our church, either by preaching, remonstrances,
warnings, declarations, acts or petitions of church judicatories, or
any other way; and to compose themselves to that quietness and
inoffensive deportment which their duty to us and the good of the
church doth require.'[1]   In Parliament itself no one dared to utter
a sound that was not in consonance with the royal will.[2]

The way being now prepared for the contemplated change in
church government, a royal letter, dated 14th August 1661, is laid
before the Privy Council on the 5th September; and on the following
day the Council pass an Act and Proclamation (which is an echo of
the King's letter) introducing Episcopacy.[3]   The King commences his
letter by referring to his letter just a year before addressed to the
Presbytery of Edinburgh, in which he had declared it his purpose to
maintain the government of the Church of Scotland, 'as settled by
law;' and now (it would seem quite in accordance with this purpose)
he makes known his 'firm resolution to interpose our royal authority
for restoring to that church its right government by bishops as it
was by law, before the late troubles, during the reigns of our royal
father and grandfather of blessed memory, and as it now stands
settled by law.'   There is no doubt that by the phrase, 'settled by
law,' in his letter to the Presbytery of Edinburgh, the King led them
to understand the Acts establishing *their* church, while at the very
time he was regarding these Acts as 'null and void,' even before
they had been set aside by the Act Rescissory, and was looking to
the Acts (really set aside, and not yet restored) establishing Prelacy.
in the previous reign.

It is not of the least importance to inquire whether King Charles
was himself guilty of this unkingly deception, or whether it was the
act of another.   Sharp was at Court when both letters were written.
One thing is clear, that Prelacy was introduced into Scotland, not
only by an act of absolute authority, without consultation with the
church, but under cover of a mean equivocation.   Yet, notwithstanding all this, the Presbyterians did not cast off their allegiance, and
rebel.   They merely craved the liberty of petitioning, of which they
had been deprived.

In the end of the year 1661, four Scotch prelates were consecrated
in London, and they, on their return, consecrated six others to fill up
the episcopate.

The Parliament (of which the new bishops were influential mem-

---

[1] Wodrow, vol. i. p. 151.

[2] The Privy Council Minutes, 13th September 1661, show that, in consequence of
a letter from the King, the Earl of Tweeddale is committed to the Castle of Edinburgh,
merely because of the King 'having received information of some speeches uttered by
him' in the trial of Mr. James Guthrie, which his Majesty was 'informed did tend
much to the prejudice of our authority.'

[3] Wodrow, vol. i. p. 230.

bers) commenced its second session on the 8th May 1662. The first Act passed was 'for the restitution and re-establishment of the ancient government of the church by archbishops and bishops.'[1] This was followed by other Acts, all designed to uphold and defend the newly erected hierarchy. Only two of these need be referred to. An 'Act concerning such benefices and stipends as have been possessed without presentations from the lawful patrons,'[2] ordains that ministers who entered their charges in or since the year 1649 shall have no right to the fruits of their benefices; but their places, benefices, and kirks shall be vacant unless they shall ask a presentation from the patron, and *obtain collation from the bishop of the diocese* before the 20th September of the current year. Another Act—'Act concerning masters of universities, ministers, etc.'[3]—ordains that no one can hold an office in a university who does not submit to and own the government of the church now settled by law; and that all ministers who do not attend the diocesan meetings, and thus acknowledge their bishop, shall, for the first offence, be suspended, and if they 'amend not,' be deprived of church and benefice.

When this second session of Parliament ended in September, the Council lost no time in putting the above-mentioned Acts into execution. On the 10th September they passed an Act 'anent diocesan meetings,'[4] fixing the times of meeting, and ordering the attendance of the clergy, under pain of incurring the censures provided in such cases. Thereafter, the Commissioners—Middleton, and a full quorum of Council—proceeded to Glasgow, where, on the 1st October (in the midst of much jollity, it is said), they passed the famous Act (known as the Glasgow Act), which prohibits and discharges all ministers who have not, according to the Act concerning benefices, obtained collation from the bishop, 'to exercise any part of the function of their ministry at their respective churches in time coming, which are hereby declared vacant;' the people are forbidden to attend their ministry, under pain of being punished; the ministers are charged to remove out of their several parishes before the 1st November, and 'not to reside within the bounds of their respective presbyteries.'[5] Though, by a subsequent Act of Council, the time allowed for complying with the terms of the Act anent benefices was extended to the 1st February following, about 200 parishes became vacant in one day by the operation of this law; and the Act requiring attendance at the diocesan meetings created vacancies in about 150 other parishes.

It was no easy matter to find qualified ministers for so many parishes; and if we may receive the testimony of Bishop Burnet (who was himself minister of Salton, in East Lothian, from 1665 to 1669), the new incumbents formed a sad contrast to those whom they succeeded. 'They were,' he says, 'generally very mean and despicable in all respects. They were the worst preachers I ever heard; they

---

[1] Wodrow, vol. i. p. 257.
[2] *Ibid.*, vol. i. p. 265.
[3] *Ibid.*, vol. i. p. 266.
[4] *Ibid.*, vol. i. p. 280.
[5] *Ibid.*, vol. i. p. 282.

were ignorant to a reproach, and many of them were openly vicious. They were a disgrace to their orders and the sacred functions, and were indeed the dregs and refuse of the northern parts.' Of the ejected ministers, he says that they 'had lived in so decent a manner that the gentry paid great respect to them;' and he bears testimony to the diligence and success of their ministry by saying, that even cottagers and servants 'had a comprehension of matters of religion greater than I have seen among people of that sort anywhere.'[1] Sir Walter Scott[2] and Principal Lee,[3] both thoroughly conversant with the history of that period, contrast the new and the old incumbents in equally strong language.

The consequence of this state of things was, that the people, as a matter of course, deserted the parish churches, and attended the ministrations of their ejected pastors. This soon led to severe laws being passed, not only against 'conventicles,' as such meetings for religious worship were termed, but also against *mere nonconformity*— the not attending worship in the parish church.

So early as the 23d December 1662, an Act of Council imposes a fine of twenty shillings Scots on each person for each time he absents himself, without lawful excuse, from his own parish church;[4] and the Parliament which met in June following passed (10th July) an 'Act against separation and disobedience to ecclesiastical authority'[5] (usually styled the Bishops' drag-net), which ordains, that if any of the ejected ministers 'shall hereafter presume to exercise their ministry,' they shall be 'punished as seditious persons;' that all persons 'who shall hereafter ordinarily and wilfully withdraw and absent themselves from the ordinary meetings of divine worship in their own parish church, on the Lord's day (whether upon account of Popery or other disaffection to the present government of the church), shall thereby incur the pains and penalties underwritten:' which penalties are, for each heritor, the fourth of the rent of the year in which he shall be convicted; for each tenant, a fourth of his free moveables; for each burgess, to lose the liberty of his burgh, and a fourth of his moveables. The execution of this Act is committed to the Privy Council, who are 'to call before them all such persons as, after admonition of the ministers, in presence of two sufficient witnesses, and by him so attested, shall be given up to the Council as transgressors.' The Council, upon conviction, may inflict the above penalties, 'and such other corporal punishment as they shall think fit.'

This Act of Parliament against nonconformity was followed by a stringent Act and Proclamation of Council (dated 13th August) against conventicles.[6] This has been termed the *Mile Act*. It charges all ministers, who, without obtaining institution from the bishop of the

[1] *Burnet's Own Times*, vol. i. p. 156.   [2] *History of Scotland*, vol. ii. pp. 10, 12.
[3] *History of the Church of Scotland*, vol. ii. p. 322.
[4] Wodrow, vol. i. p. 285.   [5] *Ibid.*, vol. i. p. 350.
[6] *Ibid.*, vol. i. p. 340.

diocese, 'have, notwithstanding, continued to preach or exercise any duty proper to the function of the ministers, either at these parish churches where they were incumbents, *or at any other place, house, or family,* to remove themselves, their families, and goods belonging to them, within twenty days after publication hereof, out of those respective parishes where they were incumbents, and not to reside within twenty miles of the same, nor within six miles of Edinburgh, or any cathedral church, or three miles of any burgh royal within this kingdom.' If they fail to give 'exact obedience,' they are 'to incur the penalties of the laws against movers of sedition, and to be proceeded against with that strictness that is due to so great contempts of his Majesty's authority over church and state.' By this same Proclamation, all heritors and householders who should give 'any presence or countenance' to such ministers, are warned that they will 'be proceeded against according to law.'

After 1663, there was no meeting of Parliament for several years, but the Privy Council continued to issue its Acts and Proclamations. One of these 'against conventicles'[1] (7th December 1665) may be noticed. All persons who 'shall be present at such unlawful meetings shall be looked upon as seditious persons, and shall be punished by fining, confining, and other corporal punishments.' Such ministers as 'shall dare to perform any acts of the ministerial function,' and all who reset them, shall be liable, not only to the foresaid pains, but also to the highest pains which may by law be inflicted on seditious persons.

A subsequent Act of Council (11th October 1666), passed in obedience to a royal letter,[2] makes masters answerable for their families and servants, requires landlords to take bonds from their tenants, and magistrates of burghs from the inhabitants, as a security that they will frequent the worship of the parish church, and abstain from conventicles.

Let it be noticed, that all the above Acts and Proclamations were passed *before any overt act of rebellion had taken place, except withdrawing from the parish church, and worshipping elsewhere.*

Nor were the laws against church offences allowed to lie a dead letter. They were all along in the hands of a vigorous executive. The records of the Privy Council show the diligence used in ejecting such ministers as had not owned the bishops within the time allowed them. Among many similar cases, a minute of 24th February 1663 shows, that *twenty-five ministers of the Synod of Galloway* were charged to remove from their parishes (and not reside within the bounds of their presbyteries) before the 20th March, and to appear before the Council on the 24th March, 'to answer for their former disobedience.'

But the best proof that there was to be a vigorous execution of the newly framed laws, is found in the erection of a new tribunal for that purpose (16th January 1664). This was the *Court of High Commission,* consisting of *nine* prelates and *thirty-five* other members,—

[1] Wodrow, vol. i. p. 430.   [2] *Ibid.*, vol. ii. p. 15.

five members to form a quorum, provided one of them were a bishop.[1]
We believe there are no records of the proceedings of this court extant, and consequently but few of its acts have got into history. But
there can be no doubt, from the terms of its appointment, viz. to 'put
in vigorous and impartial execution' the Acts of Parliament and Council
in behalf of the government of the church, that it was a severe and
arbitrary tribunal, designed to punish the breakers of the church laws
by the shortest process, without being fettered by 'the usual formalities
and maxims of law.' It is said that the lay members were so shocked
at the cruelty of the bishops, that they refused to act with them.
Whether this was the case or not, the Commission was allowed to expire
at the end of the second year.

Under the Privy Council, and the High Commission while it
lasted, the *army* and the *clergy* were the chief agencies employed to
execute the laws against transgressors. Soldiers were sent to those
parts of the country where the church laws were disregarded, to enforce the penalties incurred, and to execute, in whatever way they
were required, the orders of the Council or Commission. Sir James
Turner and Sir William Bannatyne commanded the troops in Galloway.
A Council minute of 24th November 1663 shows how well, at that
date, the Council were satisfied with Sir James' proceedings. They
'recommend it to the Earl of Linlithgow to write a letter of thanks to
Sir James Turner, for his care and pains taken in seeing the laws anent
church government receive due obedience ; and withal, to acquaint him
that he advise with the Bishop of Galloway, and send a note to the
Council of the names of such ministers as are come in from Ireland
to that country, or others who transgress, by preaching, or otherwise, the Acts of Parliament and Council, anent the government of
the church.' Wodrow, commenting on this, says, 'This person' (Sir
James) 'was abundantly ready to execute the orders here given him
with rigour, but was obliged to go even beyond his inclinations to
satisfy the Bishop of Galloway, who was severe and cruel.' Some
will say that this is one of Wodrow's 'calumnies,' which rest on no
better authority than the accounts of 'sufferings' given in by Presbyterians. But it so happens that, in this instance, the substantial truth
of Wodrow's character of the bishop can be proved by no less an
authority than the bishop himself. The records of his synodical
meetings are still extant, the original manuscript (in the handwriting
of Mr. Andrew Symson, minister of Kirkinner, clerk of synod) having
been discovered in 1847 by the late Principal Lee, in an old-book
shop in Edinburgh. These interesting records, now in the hands of
the clerk of the Synod of Galloway, have been published.[2] As they

---

[1] Wodrow, vol. i. p. 384.

[2] *The Registers of the Synod of Galloway*, from October 1664 to April 1671.
Kirkcudbright. Printed and published by J. Nicholson, 1856.

Principal Lee, in his letter to the Synod of Galloway (12th April 1847), in presenting
the manuscript, says of it: 'It is in the well-known handwriting of Mr. Andrew Symson,
minister of Kirkinner, the synod clerk, an office for which he was better fitted than for

are not much known, an extract or two may be given, to vindicate Wodrow, and to illustrate the execution of the church laws in the early years of the struggle, and while as yet only passive resistance had been offered.

The bishop and synod met at Wigtown 25th October 1664, and on the following day passed an '*Act anent such as separate from the public ordinances:*'—

'The which day it was represented to the Bishop and Synod, by divers Ministers present, that many of their Parishioners did willfully absent themselves from ye preaching of the word and other divine ordinances, and did refuse to bring their children to the Church to be baptized by them, but either keeped them unbaptized, or took them to outed Ministers of their owne principles to be baptized privately by them: Therefore ye Bishop and Synod ordains all ye Ministers within this Diocese of Galloway to take notice of such persons as have absented themselves hitherto from their Churches and other divine ordinances, and conform not to the Act of Counsell made for remeid hereof, and to admonish all such persons in their severall parishes to keep ye Church, and that upon three severall Lord's days in time of divine service; and in case, after the said three admonitions, they shall continue obstinate, to delate and present their names to the Bishop, that letters may be raised to cite them before ye High Commission, to be punished for this their contempt of ye ordinances, and of the laws of Church and State made for observing of the same. As also, because it was thought nether possible nor necessary that all ye common people of a parish who willfully absents themselves from Church should be cited to ye High Commission, or that honourable judicatorie should be troubled with such a multitude of common people as might be brought before them upon that account, the Bishop and Synod, considering seriously what course were left to be taken for curing of the obstinate spirits of such persons, and finding that the lenity that hitherto hath been used towards them hath rather encouraged them to go on in contempt of divine ordinances than been a meanes to amend them: Therefore the Bishop and Synod thinks it fit that their obstinacy should be represented to ye Lords of his Majesty's Secret Counsell, and their Lordships humbly desired to lead in a party of souldiers to quarter upon such obstinate persons in every parish as shall be nominate to them by the Minister thereof, until they pay twenty shillings Scots for every day's absence from ye Church, conform to the Act of Counsell made thereanent, and because several persons in several parishes have been already admonished three several Lord's days, the Bishop and Synod ordains the Ministers thereof to send their names, attested under their hands, to the Bishop, that letters may be raised for summoning them to the High Commission in the interim. And likewise, because the Bishop and Synod finds that several ministers have been somewhat too sparing hitherto to admonish such obstinate delinquents, or, being admonished, to present their names to ye effect foresaid: Therefore it is hereby ordained that they shall, immediately after their return to their severall Churches, put this present Act to execution according to the true intent and meaning thereof, without any respect or favour to any person or persons of whatever degree, quality, or sex they be of. Discharging ye saids Ministers and every one of them, under the paine of ye highest censure, to conceal or dispense with any such delinquents, unless they do presently come to the Church and give full assurance for keeping of ye same in all time coming. Ordaining ye severall Presbyteries and Moderators of this Diocese to take coppies of this present Act, and to cause every Minister within their bounds to make public intimation of the same in their severall Churches so soone as conveniently may be.'

The synod met at Kirkcudbright 25th April 1666, Sir James

the functions either of a poet or historian.' We have seen the manuscript, and have no doubt of its genuineness, having seen Mr. Symson's handwriting and signature in his list of parishioners, in the Register House, Edinburgh.

B

Turner being then in town, when several Acts were passed, of which the following may be given as a specimen : ' *Anent such Ministers within ye bounds of the Presbytery of Kirkcudbright as do either abet or keep Conventicles :*'—

' The day foresaid ye Bishop and Synod appoints Mr. Patrick Swinton, Mr. William Naysmith, and Mr. Alexander Irwin to represent to Sir James Turner, being now in town, the names of such Ministers within the bounds of the Presbytery of Kirkcudbright as do either abet or keep Conventicles, and to desire him to take such course as may remeid ye same. Their names are as followeth—viz. Mr. Adam Alison, Mr. John Wilkie, Mr. Samuel Arnot, Mr. James Buglasse, Mr. Alexander Robertson, Mr. William Hay, Mr. John Cant, Mr. Thomas Verner, and Mr. John Blicater.'

This is followed by an ' *Act anent ye late Ministers abiding in places by law prohibited :*'—

' The Bishop and Synod, taking into serious consideration, that although ye late Ministers do reside within places prohibited to them by law, yet, notwithstanding, they do altogether dishaunt the public ordinances of Christ within these parishes where they abide, which practise of theirs tends to the great stumbling of some and disheartening of others : Therefore ye Bishop and Synod ordains ye several Presbyteries within ye Diocese of Galloway, betwixt ye date hereof and the first term of Whitsunday next to come, to put in execution these letters of horning delivered to last Synod, and not to sist in the least unless they frequent ye ordinances according to law.'

On the same day two other Acts are passed. The first is ' *Anent a Band to be tendered to willfull Withdrawers and Conventicle Keepers :*'—

' The Bishop and Synod condiscends anent ye overture offered by Sir James Turner, that a Band be tendered by every Minister to their disorderly Parishioners, wherein they are to oblige themselves, under penalty (suteable to their qualities), for observing ye ordinances in time coming, dishaunting of Conventicles, not countenancing or resetting in their families seditious preachers ; and ye Bishop and Synod ordains that the diligence of the severall Ministers anent the subscribers of ye said Bands, with the names of such as refuse to subscribe ye samen, be returned to Sir James Turner against ye fifteen day of May next to come. And the Bishop and Synod appoints Mr. Patrick Swinton, Mr. George Davidson, Mr. William Naysmith, Mr. Alexander Irwin, and Mr. James Colhoun, to go to Sir James Turner and give him the thanks of ye Synod, as also to advise with him anent the draught of the Band forsaid, and to report to next session.'

The other is an ' *Act for delateing willfull Withdrawers and Conventicle Keepers :*'—

' The Bishop and Synod requires and commands ye severall Ministers within this Diocese to give in an exact and impartial list of all willfull and ordinary Withdrawers, Conventicle Keepers, and abetters of ye same that are within their respective congregations unto the Synod at their next session.'

Accordingly, it appears that at the next session the draught of a bond to be tendered to disorderly persons is given in, approved of, and ordered to be used; and at the same time the several ministers gave in lists of their withdrawers and conventicle keepers, ' which lists were delivered to the Bishop.'

These records of the Bishop of Galloway's proceedings (for the clergy under him were but his humble instruments) show that

Wodrow's character of the bishop was not very far from the truth, and they give grounds for believing that the sufferings of the Presbyterians could not be altogether fabulous. With such laws and such an executive, there must needs have been sufferings. The High Commission, we may be certain, was not idle, though it has left no record of its proceedings; and the Council records (besides the numerous processes against individuals which they show) make us aware of the significant fact, that the two commanders in Galloway were prosecuted for their severities. Sir James Turner, who in 1663 was thanked for his services by the Council, and in 1666 by the Bishop of Galloway, was, in consequence of a letter from the King, dated 26th November 1667,[1] brought before the Council for his excesses in executing the church laws, and dismissed the service.[2] Sir William Bannatyne seems to have carried his severities still farther, for by an Act of Council[3] (4th August 1668) he was not only dismissed the service, but fined and banished.

With such facts before us, just as they appear in public documents and records, even had we no other sources of proof, we may judge whether Mr. Napier is correct or not when he says: ' At no time was it the inclination or system of the Restoration Governments to punish old or young for merely holding Covenanting opinions, and being attached to the anti-Prelatic form of church government and worship.' [4] Not only the laws enacted, but the measures taken to ensure their execution, clearly show the contrary, even during the earlier years of the Restoration rule, when no arm had been raised against the Government.

The rising that commenced, without premeditation or concert, at Dalry, in Galloway, on 13th November 1666, and terminated disastrously for the insurgents at Pentland on the 28th of that month, showed that, notwithstanding their cruel oppression, the people generally were averse to join the standard of rebellion. But now there were in the land those who, having borne arms against the Government, were termed ' rebels.' Of the hundred and thirty taken prisoners, about one-half were executed as traitors, and the rest banished. Of those who escaped, the greater number, refusing the offered terms of indemnity, were thenceforth pursued as fugitives and outlaws.

In the following year (1667) there were appearances of a milder rule. Lauderdale was now at the head of affairs in Scotland, and the bishops had less influence in the Council. Hyde, the English Chancellor (Lord Clarendon), who, being the great patron of High Church principles in England, exerted, it is thought, an evil influence on Scotch affairs, had fallen from his place of power. The army was now for a time withdrawn from the south and west. Some of the

---

[1] Wodrow, vol. ii. p. 101.

[2] When Sir James settled accounts with the Government, he owned that he had received 30,000 pounds Scots of church fines; which statement was accepted, because it was impossible to prove the larger sum charged against him.

[3] Wodrow, vol. ii. p. 104.　　　　　[4] *Case for the Crown*, p. 119.

commanders of the troops, as we have noticed above, were called to
account for the severities they had exercised under the instructions of
the bishops and synods ; an *Indulgence* was granted by Government to
certain of the outed ministers to exercise their ministry, under certain
conditions, in places to which they were appointed by the Council ;
and they were even allowed a stipend, of a small amount, out of the
revenues of the church.   Bishop Leighton, too, doubtless with consent
of those in power, proposed an *Accommodation* to the Presbyterian
ministers.   But neither the *Indulgence* nor the *Accommodation* found
much favour with the ministers, and still less with the people—both
being looked upon as lures to draw them by degrees to the acknow-
ledgment of Prelacy.   The *indulged* ministers were generally despised
by the people ; and this device, which was intended to supply them
with such religious teaching as would satisfy them, and so put a stop
to conventicles, entirely failed in its object.

In the year 1670—from what cause it is difficult to discover—
the severe measures of the Government were renewed.   The Acts of the
Parliament and the records of the Council show that there was to be
no relaxation of the laws against ecclesiastical offences.   By the Parliament of this year an ' Act anent deponing '[1] awards ' fining, close
imprisonment, or banishment,' for *not deponing* as to conventicles, or
the resetting or intercommuning with rebels.   An ' Act anent field
conventicles '[2] lays down the penalties which are to fall on those who
officiate at them, and on those who are present.   An outed minister
who preaches or prays in any meeting in *a house*, except to his own
family, is to be imprisoned till he ' find caution, under the pain of five
thousand merks, not to do the like thereafter,' or else to ' enact ' himself ' to remove out of the kingdom,' and not return without the King's
leave.   But if the above offence be committed in *the fields*, or even in
a house when some of 'the congregation are without doors, this ' shall
be punished with death, and confiscation of their goods.'   Every person present at such meetings is liable to be imprisoned till he shall
pay the fines imposed, which, in case of an heritor attending a field
conventicle, is the half of his yearly rent.   This Act, too, holds out a
reward of five hundred merks to any who shall seize the minister who
officiates at a field conventicle, and assures him of indemnity ' for any
slaughter that shall be committed in the apprehending.'   Besides, for
the ' encouragement ' of Sheriffs and other magistrates ' to be careful
and diligent in their duties,' his Majesty ' doth allow to themselves all
the fines of any persons within their jurisdiction, under the degree of
heritors.'   And, as a further hint to make good use of so favourable a
chance of filling their pockets, it is intimated that the endurance of
this Act ' shall only be for three years,' unless it be renewed.

The Parliament of this year also passed an ' Act anent separation,'[3]
which ordains that every person who, without a reasonable excuse,
shall be absent from church for three Lord's days together, shall, for
each such offence, be liable to the following penalties, viz. : An

[1] Wodrow, vol. ii. p. 167.   [2] *Ibid.*, vol. ii. p. 169.   [3] *Ibid.*, vol. ii. p. 174.

heritor, an eighth of his yearly rent; a tenant, six pounds Scots; a cottar or servant, forty shillings Scots; and so on.   If an heritor shall withdraw from church for a year, he is to be delated to the Council, who are to require him to subscribe a bond, which, if he refuses to do, he is to be secured or banished, and the liferent of his estate forfeited. The execution of this Act also is committed to Sheriffs and other local magistrates, who (as in the last noticed Act) are *encouraged* to do their duty by being allowed to pocket all the fines they inflict, except those of heritors.   Magistrates, too, are to be called to account by the Council, who may punish their negligence 'as they shall judge fit.'

On the legislation of this year Mr. Napier remarks: 'Conventicles were prohibited, and the preaching at them, and frequenting and following them was denounced and endeavoured to be crushed by an impolitic *brutum fulmen* of legislation in 1670, that was never intended to be practically followed out.'[1]   Why, then, offer a bribe to magistrates to execute these laws, and hold an arbitrary punishment by the Council, *in terrorem*, over their heads if they fail to do so?   Above all, why hold out a tempting reward to every mean informer for the capture of a conventicle preacher, and assure him of impunity if, in doing this, he should commit ' *slaughter?* '   The Council minutes of the following years furnish abundant evidence that these laws *were* followed out.   And there is no doubt they were generally enforced in the local courts.   If it was the case that some of the magistrates did not execute them with rigour, it was not because they were so instructed by the Government.   The hereditary Sheriffs of Galloway were lenient, comparatively, to offenders against the church laws. The consequence was, that in 1677 Sir Andrew Agnew, the tenth of his line who had held the office of sheriff, was ordered by the Council to appoint as his deputes John Graham of Claverhouse, and the Lairds of Lagg and Earlshall, to insure a stricter administration of the law.[2] If the people of Galloway, under the administration of the laws by the Agnews, held views similar to Mr. Napier's as to the intentions of the Government, they probably came to a different opinion when they made the acquaintance of Claverhouse and the other new deputes in the Sheriff Court.

By a proclamation of the Council, 2d August 1677, heritors were required to give *bonds* that they would prevent, not only their families and domestics, but also their tenants and dependants, from attending all interdicted meetings.   To enforce this order, which was generally resisted as unreasonable, besides a large number of regular troops, the 'Highland Host' (the wild clans from the north), to the number of 6000, were sent down to desolate the west and south, by quartering on the inhabitants, extorting money, and carrying off everything that was valuable.   'When the Highlanders,' says Sir Walter Scott, ' went back to their hills, which was in February 1678, they appeared as if returning from the sack of some besieged town.'[3]

[1] *Case for the Crown*, p. 119.   [2] *Hereditary Sheriffs*, p. 384.
[3] *History of Scotland*, vol. ii. p. 31.

These severe measures of the Government, in place of suppressing rebellion, tended only to multiply the rebels, to increase discontent, and to extinguish loyalty. The rebels and outlaws, who were cut off from society, and hunted for their lives, like wild beasts, in the moors and mountains, could not fail to acquire a ferocity of character which fitted them for desperate deeds in the way of reprisal; and in the case of the Primate, and of others whom they looked upon as the authors of their sufferings, they did indeed take a terrible vengeance. But these instances of reprisal were rare; and they were the acts of *individuals*, with which the general body of the Presbyterians had nothing to do, and of which they did not approve. Still, the assassination of the Primate was the occasion of increased severity in the treatment of all who were known to be hostile to the policy of the Government.

It has been maintained by some, that the measures of the Government were intended to provoke open rebellion. At all events, they tended to do so; and the gathering at Bothwell, in 1679, though as ill concerted as the rising of Pentland, and far more disastrous to the insurgents, shows clearly how the spirit of rebellion had increased. 'Three or four hundred were killed on the field. Twelve hundred surrendered at discretion, some of whom were executed, and the remainder confined five months in Greyfriars' Churchyard, without covering to shelter them from the inclemency of the weather. Several hundreds were shipped for the American plantations, but the vessel was wrecked in the Orkneys; and though they might all have been saved, the master of the ship closed the hatches upon them, so that more than two hundred perished. This savage, who had contracted to transport them for a certain sum, was afterwards indemnified by the Government for the loss of his vessel; and suspicions were entertained that, in devoting his prisoners to death, he acted agreeably to his instructions.'[1]

In consequence of this rising, forfeitures and confiscations were multiplied to enrich the servants of the Government. Claverhouse got his share of the spoil, and became a Wigtownshire laird. Patrick M'Dowall of Freuch, who had been driven from his house by the Highland Host, joined the rising. He was tried and attainted; and the forfeited lands of Freuch were granted by the Crown to Claverhouse, in consideration of his good services and 'sufferings.'[2]

'An indemnity'[3] was published after Bothwell; but it contained many exceptions; and even those who might avail themselves of it were required to 'enact themselves' never again to offer resistance to the Government, or to attend conventicles,—in fact, to renounce the principles for which they had been hitherto contending, and to accept those of their rulers.

In 1681 a new Parliament was summoned, and met in July, the Duke of York, the King's brother, being Commissioner. Former Acts

[1] Principal Lee's *History of the Church of Scotland*, vol. ii. p. 340.
[2] *Hereditary Sheriffs*, p. 386.   [3] Wodrow, vol. iii. p. 118.

anent religion were ratified;[1] and an Act was passed settling the succession to the Crown, evidently to meet the case of the Popish heir-apparent.[2] 'An Act for securing the peace of the country'[3] made the law against conventicles still more stringent, not only doubling the fines, but obliging heritors and masters to pay the fines of tenants and servants, if these possessed goods sufficient to meet the same; otherwise to dismiss them immediately from their lands or service, notwithstanding any lease or bargain. But the most important Act of this year was the *Test Act*,[4] passed 31st August, imposing an oath to be taken by all persons in public trust, but which, apparently without legal authority, was tendered generally to people even of the humblest classes. This oath was so inconsistent in its terms, that no one who understood it could take it with a good conscience. It was refused even by many who favoured the Government; and to impose this test upon a conscientious Presbyterian was to bind him, by oath, to give up what he believed to be right; to cease opposing the policy of those who were trampling under foot both civil and religious freedom; and to make, in short, the will of the Sovereign his only rule of acting in all matters both of religion and of politics.

Sir Andrew Agnew, the Sheriff of Galloway, refusing to take the test, was deprived of his office, which was bestowed upon Claverhouse on 19th January 1682; and that Claverhouse's services might not be confined entirely to this too narrow sphere, his brother, David Graham, was appointed conjoint Sheriff on the 12th May of the same year.

Claverhouse's commission from the Government[5] shows that it was expected of him that he should put the church laws in 'vigorous execution;' and his letters to headquarters, which Mr. Napier has done good service in publishing, show with what zeal he entered on his duties, and that the *ladies* of Wigtownshire were to receive from him due attention. On the 5th March 1682, he writes from Wigtown to the Marquis of Queensberry, then at the head of affairs: 'Here, in this shire, I find the lairds all following the example of a late great man and considerable heritor among them; which is to live regularly themselves, but have their houses constant haunts of rebels and intercommuned persons, and have their children baptized by the same, and then lay all the blame upon their wives. But I am resolved the jest shall pass no longer here, for it is laughing and fooling the Government.'

The Restoration Governments seem to have regarded an *oath* as a sovereign remedy for disaffection and disloyalty; so they appear to have subjected the whole male population to the test oath. A commission was given to David Graham, William Coltron (Provost of Wigtown), and Sir Godfrey M'Culloch, 'for tendering the test to the gentrie and commons within the shyre of Wigtown;' and by the end

[1] Wodrow, vol. iii. p. 290.   [2] *Ibid.*, vol. iii. p. 291.
[3] *Ibid.*, vol. iii. p. 293.   [4] *Ibid.*, vol. iii. p. 295.
[5] *Ibid.*, vol. iii. p. 370.

of 1683 they were able to report, that 'the haill gentrie and heritors within the said shyre had taken the test in the way and manner appoynted by Act of Parliament, except Sir Andrew Agnew of Lochnaw; James Agnew, his son; William M'Dowall of Garthland; William Gordon of Craichlaw; (George) Stewart of Tonderghie; Mr. Kennedy, minister in Ireland; Mr. James Laurie, who lives in Ayr; Alex. Laurie, his son; Wm. and David Gordon, sons to the said Craichlaw.'[1] But such was the pressure brought to bear upon those who declined the test, that the above-named gentlemen were constrained to yield; and they appeared before a Royal Commission, who came to hold court in Wigtown in October 1684, and took the required oath. The Commissioners were enabled then to report: 'We do therefore declare, that the haill gentrie and heritors within the shyre have taken the test, except Kennedy, minister in Ireland, and Mr. James Laurie: we further declare, that all the commons in the said shyre who had not taken the test has now done the same, except six or seven qhoo are now prisoners.' It is not easy to estimate the suffering and the sin which this statement discloses,—the inhabitants of a county forced to swear a solemn oath against their convictions.

Itinerant Commissions of Justiciary had now become common. The Privy Council and the Court of Justiciary in Edinburgh were as busy as possible, as their records show; but they could not overtake the work of punishment. Hence Commissions were appointed to traverse the country. Wodrow says that he can meet with 'no registers of these itinerant courts.'[2] He has been careful, however, to give in full, from the Council records, the Commissions appointing them, and the instructions given to them; from which any one may see what severe and arbitrary tribunals they were.

The Commission of October 1684 was an important one.[3] Different sets of Commissioners traversed the whole south and west, and it is said that about 2000 fugitives were prosecuted.[4] The Commissioners for the counties of Dumfries, Kirkcudbright, and Wigtown, were the Marquis of Queensberry, Lord Drumlanrig, and Claverhouse; and the records of their proceedings at Dumfries on the 3d and 4th October, and at Kirkcudbright on the 10th and 11th October, with lists of the persons libelled, and the original sentences, signed by the Commissioners, are now in the Register House, Edinburgh. They arrived at Wigtown on the 14th October, and the original record of their proceedings there is still in the possession of Sir Andrew Agnew, who, in his work on the *Hereditary Sheriffs*, has given some account of this curious document, and published several of the cases in it as a specimen. Through Sir Andrew's courtesy we have been permitted to

[1] *Hereditary Sheriffs*, p. 399.

[2] Records of several of these Commissions are now in the Register Office, Edinburgh. In addition to those of Dumfriesshire, the stewartry of Kirkcudbright, and a portion of Wigtownshire, there are extant those of Moray 'between the Spey and Ness,' and those of Roxburgh and the border counties.

[3] Wodrow, vol. iv. pp. 113–115.   [4] Principal Lee's *History*, vol. ii. p. 342.

examine this record. Almost all the heritors of the shire were in attendance, ' to give suit and presence to the Lords:' the few who were absent were fined. The judicial work commenced on the 16th, on which day *fifty-five* cases were disposed of. The process was of course a very summary one. No jury was empanelled, nor witness called, in any case. The party was generally sworn, interrogated, and judged on his own declaration or deposition. Most of the cases were for converse with rebels, generally accidentally. When this was admitted, and a promise, upon oath, given not in future to reset or converse, the test was administered, and the party set free. Some would not take the test or swear any oath ; some owned being at conventicles, and having had children baptized by Presbyterian ministers ; some owned converse with rebels who were near relatives, but would not depone where and when they last saw them. All these were in the meantime sent to prison, some of them in irons. Next day sentence was passed upon the prisoners ; several were banished to the plantations, and others, whose crimes were thought more aggravated, had their cases referred to the Justiciary Court in Edinburgh.

The cases of the *female* criminals who were before this Commission, we give in the terms of the record :—

' Margaret Gordon, goodwife of Arioland, elder, confesses resett of Mr. Wm. and John Hayes, her sons ; and that Mr. Samuel Arnot had kept conventicles in her house ; and being interrogat if she harboured or resett any rebel or other fugitive, or heard any more vagrant preachers, refuses to depone.

' Committed to prison.

(Signed)   ' QUEENSBERRY, I.P.D.'

' Margaret Milligan, spouse to James Martison, and Sara Stewart, spouse to William Kennedy, and Margaret M'Lurg, spouse to Alexander M'Clingan, rebells. Margaret Milligan and Margaret M'Lurg confesses the harbour of their husbands within this year and this half, but refuses to depone if they were there sensyne ; the said Sara Stewart confesses harbour of her husband within this quarter of a year, and that she has a chyld of a year old unbaptized, and is content that Mr. James Cahoun baptize her chyld, and she will hold the chyld up herself ; and is ordered to enact herself in common form, and find caution that the chyld shall be baptized.

' Milligan and M'Lurg committed to prison ; Sara Stewart enacted.

(Signed)   ' QUEENSBERRY, I.P.D.'

Next day they are brought up for sentence.

' List of woman panells whoe refuse to depone anent harbouring, conversing, and entertaining of rebells, and are secured :

' Margaret Gordon, goodwife of Arioland, elder.
    Margaret Milligan, spouse to James Martison, rebell.
    Margaret M'Lurg, spouse to Alexander M'Clingan, rebell.

'The Lords Commissioners having considered the confessions of the above-named Margaret Gordon, Margaret Milligan, and Margaret M'Lurg, and they refusing to depone anent harbour, converse, etc., decerns, adjudges, and ordains them to be banished to the plantations, and to remain prisoners in the meintyme till a fitt occasion offers for that effect.[1]

(Signed) ,   'QUEENSBERRY, I.P.D.'

'WIGTOWN, 17 Oct. 1684.'

To sentence to banishment and slavery wives for speaking to their husbands, or mothers for speaking to their sons, and refusing to inform against them, was, doubtless, severity of no ordinary character ; yet it was not beyond what the statute anent deponing allowed, and was quite in accordance with the spirit of the special instructions from the Council under which this Commission was acting ; one of these instructions being, ' You shall turn out all the wives and children of the forfeited persons and fugitives from their habitations, if it shall appear that they have conversed with their parents or husbands, or if they refuse to vindicate themselves by their oath.'

The Royal Commissioners left instructions to the Sheriff and his deputes, as well as to heritors and ministers, for their guidance in bringing all offenders to justice. This document, which well illustrates the vigorous execution of the law within the province in which Claverhouse administered justice, has been published by Sir Andrew Agnew in his interesting work, to which we have already so often referred.[2]

How were the tribunals of justice at this time supplied with their numerous victims ?   In times like these there is usually no lack of sycophants.   The army was employed in this service, and so were the curates.   We have seen, in the records of the Episcopal Synod of Galloway, that in the early years of this struggle the bishop made the clergy the informers against their own parishioners.   And now, in the year 1684, we find that every parish minister in Wigtownshire (and it was the same elsewhere[3]) was obliged to give in to the authorities a

---

[1] It appears, from the Penninghame minute of sufferings, that the sentence of banishment was not executed in the case of the wives of M'Clingan and Martison (or Martin), but that they suffered a long imprisonment.   We have not been able to obtain any information regarding Mrs. Hay of Arioland (who was a daughter of Gordon of Craichlaw), but it may be presumed that, as the sentence was not executed in the case of the other two women, neither would it be in her case.   It is well known that the Hays of Arioland, in the parish of Mochrum, were utterly ruined by the persecutions of these times ; yet the session of Mochrum, in 1711, inform the presbytery that they had no ' sufferings ' to report.   This shows that the church courts were not so zealous in collecting cases of suffering as some suppose them to have been ; and that, instead of reporting imaginary cases, they did not even report all the real ones.

[2] Hereditary Sheriffs, p. 416.

[3] The lists of most of the parishes in the districts visited by the above-mentioned Commission, except those of Wigtownshire, are to be found in the Register House. Occasionally, as in Wigtownshire, the incumbents gave in complete lists of their

list of all in his parish above twelve years of age, and to point out such of them as were transgressors of the church laws, by adding to their names the word *disorderly*, or by appending to his general list a separate one of the ' withdrawers from public worship.' In our former edition we mentioned that the list of Mr. Andrew Symson, minister of Kirkinner, given in at Wigtown, 15th October 1684 (when the Commissioners were there), had been lately discovered, and is preserved in the Register House, Edinburgh ; and that in it may be found the name of *Margaret Lauchlison*, residing at Drumjargan, marked 'disorderly.' We ventured then to say, that were the *list* of Mr. James Colhoun, curate of Penninghame, discovered, in it would most probably be found the names of the Wilsons, with the same epithet affixed to them. We can *now* say that this is the fact. The Penninghame list, and indeed the lists of all the Wigtownshire parishes (Kirkinner excepted), have lately been found among Sir Andrew Agnew's papers at Lochnaw, and through Sir Andrew's kindness we have had the opportunity of fully examining them. These lists will be of great service in showing, that the men who certified the martyrdom in question in the church courts in 1711 were living in their several parishes in 1685, when it took place. In the meantime it may suffice to state, that in the Penninghame list of *withdrawers* are the names of the three children of Gilbert Wilson of Glenvernock—Margaret, Thomas, and Agnes. We subjoin, in a note, Mr. Colhoun's list of withdrawers, just as he gives it.[1] Thus pointed out, Margaret Lauchlison, Margaret Wilson, and her younger sister Agnes, were placed at the bar of a Justiciary Court that visited Wigtown in April 1685. But before that time, events occurred which placed the Presbyterians under a severer administration of law than they had hitherto experienced.

Renwick's *Apologetical Declaration*[2] was affixed to sundry market crosses and kirk doors on the 8th November 1684. This was a manifesto of the Society People (Cameronians), called forth by the now intolerable severities of the Government, intimating that they would be

parishioners, noting the disorderly ; but in other cases the lists contain merely the names of the disorderly. Many of these are very curious and locally interesting. The Carsphairn list, given in by Mr. Peter Peirson, who was murdered in the December following, is specially noteworthy. He is said to have been a bold, resolute, and daring man. If there be any truth in handwriting being an index of character, his signature is a proof of the correctness of the report ; while the significant fact that almost the whole inhabitants of his parish are returned as disorderly, explains the general detestation in which he was held, and affords a strong corroboration of the truth of Wodrow's story, and of the traditions regarding him.

[1] A list of withdrawers from public worship :—Elizabeth Gordon, Lady Castle-Stewart, and her waiting maid, Mary Ramsay, not now dwelling there. Janet Dunbar, young Lady Craichlaw, and Isabella M'Clellan, her servant. Marjory Dunbar, Lady Fintilloch. Thomas Wilson, sometyme in Glenvernock, Margaret Wilson, Agnes Wilson. In Baltersen, Elspey M'Gill, Patrick M'Clellan, Margaret Heron, widow. At the Mill of Penninghame, Helen Gordon. At Colbratton, William M'Camon, John Murdoch, sometyme in this parish.—This list subscribed by me, James Colhoun.

[2] Wodrow, vol. iv. p. 148.

compelled to resort to measures of self-defence, if any should ' stretch forth their hands against them,' and especially vowing vengeance against informers and ' intelligencers' who betray them, and those who befriend them, and bring them before the courts of their adversaries.   Shortly after the publication of this Declaration two soldiers of the Life Guard were murdered in Linlithgowshire, and the curate of Carsphairn in his manse.   These acts were of course considered by the Government as the natural result of the Declaration; but the Societies disavowed all connection with the authors of them, and cut off from their fellowship the supposed murderers of the curate.   Those who murdered the two soldiers were never even suspected.   If any one, in consequence of the Declaration, took it upon himself to take vengeance on his persecutors, he was acting contrary to its express terms; for it says, ' We abhor, condemn, and discharge any *personal attempts*, upon any pretext whatever.'   Anything in the way of reprisal was not to be done ' without previous deliberation, common or competent consent, with certain probation by sufficient witnesses, the guilty person's confession, or the notoriousness of the deeds themselves,'—not, in short, without what Sir George Mackenzie calls their ' mock courts of justice.' Though they threatened (it may be, as he says, ' ridiculously') to keep such courts, there is no proof that they ever did so; or that they condemned any one to death, and then executed the sentence.   The cases of murder (not numerous, it must be allowed) that then occurred were probably acts of personal revenge, which might have taken place all the same had no such manifesto ever been issued.   No doubt the party who issued the Declaration disavowed all loyalty to the reigning King; but in this they did only what the *nation* did a few years later. No doubt they intimated, it may be in intemperate language, their determination, should relentless persecution be continued, to resort to measures of reprisal in self-defence; but at the same time they disavowed, in equally strong terms, the persecuting principles of their adversaries : ' We do hereby,' say they, ' jointly and unanimously testify and declare, that we utterly detest and abhor that hellish principle of killing all who differ in judgment and persuasion from us.'

The Apologetical Declaration, though the manifesto of a body by no means formidable, seems to have cast the Government into a great panic.   Mr. Napier tells us that ' the King's Government became alarmed and excited.   At ten in the morning of the same day (on which the soldiers were killed) the Lord Register writes to Queensberry in such agitation that his letter can scarcely be deciphered : *For God's sake, take care of yourself;* for now that these villains are at the utmost despair, they will act as *devils*, to whom they belong.'[1] And Sir George Mackenzie, when writing his vindication some years after, says of that time, ' No man who served the King could know whether or not his murderer was at his elbow.'   If this alarm was real, and not affected, it shows how ' conscience does make cowards of us all.'   The men who had been witnessing experiments with the *boot*

[1] *Case for the Crown*, p. 23.

and the *thumbkins*,[1] and whose almost daily work had been hanging and beheading, turned pale at the possibility of danger to themselves. The receipt of what was really nothing more than a *threatening letter*, set this ' nation of gallant men and cavaliers,' the heroes of romance, but not yet of history, into a fearful excitement. So, at least, says Mr. Napier. And he is probably right ; for the measures taken to meet this threatening of ' war' were not the measures of brave and gallant men. What were their measures ? They ran in haste to the Lords of Justiciary to consult with them regarding the framing of a *new oath*, to be tendered to any whom they pleased, *even to women*, binding them not to make war upon those who served the King.

This measure of the Government claims careful attention, for it was under the law now introduced that the Wigtown sufferers were condemned. The query put by the Council to the judges is as follows :—

' Whether any of his Majesty's subjects, being questioned by his Majesty's Judges or Commissioners if they own a late Proclamation in so far as it declares war against his sacred Majesty, and asserts that it is lawful to kill all those who are employed by his Majesty, refusing to answer upon oath, are thereby guilty of high treason, and art and part in the said treasonable Declaration ? '

To this answer was given—

' It is the unanimous opinion of the Lords of Council and Session, that a libel, in terms of the said query, is relevant to infer the crime of treason, as art and part of the said treasonable Declaration, against the refusers.'

When this answer was considered by the Privy Council, there was a difference of opinion, and consequently a *vote* was taken. ' It being put to the vote in the Council whether or not any person owns, or does not disown, the late traitorous Declaration upon oath, whether they have arms or not, should be immediately killed before two witnesses, and the person or persons who are to hold instructions from the Council for that effect ? Carried in the affirmative.' No wonder that there was a vote in the Council ; for their deliverance was not in accordance with the opinion they had obtained from the judges. That opinion implied that there was to be a *libel* and a trial of some sort. But that was too slow a form of process to suit the present mood of the majority of the Council ; so they ' ordain any person who owns or will not disown the late treasonable declaration upon oath, whether they have arms or not, to be immediately put to death, this being always done in the presence of two witnesses, and the person or persons having commission from the Council for that effect.' [2] From the 22d November 1684 this was law. An officer in the army (even a very inferior one) having such commission from the Council, if accom-

[1] So late as the 23d July previous the Council had ordained, ' When any person shall by their order be put to the torture, that the said boots and thumbkins *both* be applied to them.'

[2] Wodrow, vol. iv. p. 154.

panied by two troopers, might stop the honest traveller on his way, or
the peasant in the labours of his field, and questioning him as to his
views of the Government, or of the Covenant, offer him the oath of
abjuration, and if he declined it, order him there and then to be shot.

This being the state of the law, there is nothing very improbable in
Wodrow's history of the 'killing time.' It is just what might be expected
under such legislation; and the numerous monuments which,
in Mr. Napier's eyes, desecrate the Scottish soil, may still, if the above
statute be kept in mind, be looked upon as commemorating martyrs,
and not as perpetuating a calumny. Wodrow could not report the
field executions which took place under this law, from the records of
any court of justice; but he had other sufficient evidence,—the testimony
of living witnesses,—testimony which was not disputed at the
time, and which it is too late to dispute now. But what though no
evidence of these barbarities had been preserved, and no narrative of
them written; or what though Mr. Napier should succeed in proving
them all to be fable? The law issued by the Privy Council still
stands on their records, and these records also show that they took the
means to have it enforced; so that even if there were no sufferings
and no martyrdoms such as Wodrow relates, that would not have been
owing to the wisdom, moderation, and humanity of those who then
ruled the kingdom of Scotland.[1]

The next day after the abjuration was resolved on in the Council,
a Commission was appointed for the parish of Livingstone (in which
the soldiers had been murdered) and the five adjoining ones. They
were instructed to 'convocate all the inhabitants, men and women,
above fourteen years of age.' They were to 'examine every person.'
Those who swore the abjuration were to be dismissed, if they were not
suspected of guilt. If any owned the late Declaration, or the assassination
of the soldiers, they were to be executed, 'by military execution,
upon the place.' Any who refuse to answer or depone, are to be tried
before a jury there and then; and if they refuse to abjure the Declaration,
are to be sentenced to death, and executed 'instantly.' They
were to 'seize their goods,' and they were to 'make prisoners of all
persons in their families above the age of twelve years, in order to

---

[1] Mr. Napier would have us believe that the anticipation of Argyle's invasion from
Holland had to do with the severe measures of the Government at this time. When the
Government passed their law in November 1684, they seem to have had no anticipation
of Argyle's invasion in May following. The correspondence that passed between the
members of the Government indicates no such suspicion. On the day that Renwick's
Proclamation is known to the Council, Sir George Mackenzie of Tarbat, the Lord Register,
reports the matter to Queensberry, and indicates the measures the Council meant to take.
'Since we find there is a party declaring war who *lurk within us*, we think on a
strict inquiry *for all in the nation* who will not *forswear* those opinions, and especially
in Edinburgh, and at any rate to free the kingdom of all of them; for hunting and
hawking are judged absolutely insecure.'—(*Case for the Crown*, p. 22.) The reason here
given for the *abjuration* is, not Argyle's coming, but that the gentlemen of the Council
and their friends in the country may enjoy their field sports *safely*.

transplantation.'[1]   Children under twelve years (whose parents are to be executed, and their elder brothers and sisters 'transplanted') the Council do not undertake to legislate for, but leave them, like sparrows, to the care of God's providence.

The results of this first grand trial under the new law, even as they are narrated by Wodrow, must be highly satisfactory to Mr. Napier, and in his view no blame will attach to the Government in connection with their procedure in this case.   All seem to have sworn the easily-taken abjuration, down to the small boys and girls.   No one was executed—no one was banished—no children were left orphans.   There were no martyrs; and no monuments now desecrate the soil.   But there was no discovery of the murder.   On perusing this extraordinary page of history, one cannot but wonder, if the Privy Council considered that, by this grand swearing match, they had converted these six contiguous parishes into a peaceful and loyal territory in which they might hunt and hawk, during the now approaching Christmas recess, without fear of bodily harm; or if, on the other hand, they had still a suspicion that those who would most readily abjure the principles of rebellion and assassination, would be the very persons who would most likely put them in practice.

At all events, the Government were not discouraged by the result of this first experiment with the abjuration oath.   They still followed the same policy, and Commission after Commission was sent out to traverse all parts of the country, to pledge the people to unresisting loyalty by means of the new oath.   The instructions given to these Commissions (and still to be found in the records of the Council) show the work they were expected to do, and sufficiently evince the spirit and temper of the Government.   More especially are the instructions given to the Commissioners, who were to commence their several circuits on the 15th January 1685, deserving notice; because these same instructions were to guide the Commission of which Colonel Douglas was the head, and which was issued on the 27th March 1685, in the name of King James, who had now succeeded his brother,—the Commission by which the Wigtown women were tried and sentenced. These instructions, as they stand in the Council minutes, are given at length by Wodrow.[2]   We quote the portion merely which especially refers to our present inquiry:

'2d. If any person own the principles (of Renwick's Declaration), or do not disown them, they must be judged at least by three, and you must immediately give them a libel and the names of the inquest and witnesses; and they, being found guilty, are to be hanged immediately in the place according to law.   But at this time you are not to examine any women, but such as have been active in the said courses in a signal manner, *and those are to be drowned.*'

On this statute Mr. Napier remarks: 'This was an instruction, not of barbarous cruelty, but of careful criminal justice; and as regards women, the spirit and intention was as humane as the condition of the

---

[1] Wodrow, vol. iv. p. 156.   [2] Wodrow, vol. iv. p. 165.

country could possibly admit of. However guilty, women were to be drowned simply, and not hanged as traitors or dismembered.'[1] Mr. Napier is entitled to hold his own opinion as to the *humanity* of the instructions of the Privy Council as regards women, though very few will agree with him. The fact that at this time the Government of Scotland ordered that females who would not swear the abjuration oath should be put to death by *drowning*, stands uncontradicted. 'The condition of the country,' it is said, admitted of nothing more lenient than this mild death by drowning. No doubt the country was in as bad a condition as it could be in; things had come to the worst, and were therefore about to amend. The Government that found it necessary to make women swear that they would not make war against it, was certainly reduced to its last shift, and must soon make way for a better.

No record of the proceedings at Wigtown of the Commission by which Margaret Lauchlison and Margaret and Agnes Wilson were tried, has as yet been found; but as in recent years not a few papers which cast light on this passage of history have unexpectedly turned up, it is not improbable that this interesting document may still be discovered.

The Commission granted to Colonel Douglas is quoted at length by Wodrow.[2] It gives the names of the Commissioners in the several districts (nine districts were to be visited), who were to concur with him when present, and, in his absence, any three of them to follow his instructions. The Commissioners for Kirkcudbright and Wigtown were, Lord Kenmuir, Sir Robert Grierson, Sir David Dunbar, Sir Godfrey M'Culloch, and Mr. David Graham. The officers in the army in the several districts were also in the Commission. Considering the wide field over which Colonel Douglas's Commission extended, the probability is, that he was not present at Wigtown; and the Penninghame Session minute is probably correct in stating that the judges in the case in question were, David Graham, and Lagg, with Major Winram, and Captain Strachan.

From the petition of the elder woman, Margaret Lauchlison, lately found in the Register House, Edinburgh, we learn that the Commissioners held a court at Wigtown on the 13th April 1685, and that on that day, she, and doubtless her young companion Margaret Wilson, and probably, too, Agnes Wilson, who had *all* (as we have seen proof) been informed upon as 'disorderly,' were at the bar of this circuit court. What, in their case, is implied in being *disorderly* cannot be exactly defined, but they were doubtless transgressors of the church laws, perhaps as *actively* so as an old woman and young girls could be. The old woman was living in her house in Kirkinner in October 1684, when Mr. Symson reported her, and it is said she was there when apprehended. But the young Wilsons, at the date of Mr. Colhoun's report, were *not living with their father.* Thus Mr. Colhoun confirms the Penninghame Session minute, which says that they and

[1] *Case for the Crown*, p. 26.   [2] Wodrow, vol. iv. p. 207.

their brother had 'fled, and lived in the wild mountains, bogs, and caves.' Theirs was doubtless a most 'disorderly' life. They were consorting with fugitives, and not only 'dishaunting the ordinances,' but frequenting conventicles. These two girls had really transgressed the law to their utmost ability; and the old woman, though not 'active in the said courses' herself, had likely encouraged others to be so. She may have had a persuasive eloquence, and may have made more use of that gift than, in those times, it was safe to do.

But whatever may have been the extent of their offending, they had been *delated* to the authorities, and therefore they are at the bar of this Justiciary Court. For such persons, the abjuration oath was now the Government's prescribed remedy. It was tendered to them, and refused; and the jury that sat upon them brought them in guilty. Thereupon, in strict accordance with the Privy Council's instructions, and by no arbitrary proceeding on the part of the judges, they are sentenced to be drowned. *That fact is not denied.* The judges are even more merciful than the lawgivers; for, contrary to instructions, they do not execute the sentence *immediately.* It is now denied that it was ever executed. That is now the only point in dispute. But before proceeding to look at the proof, both on the *negative* and *affirmative* sides of the question, we may ask, What gain or glory would result to the 'Crown' (the Government of the day) even should Mr. Napier succeed in proving the *negative?* It would still be true that the Government framed a law ordaining that women, who would not swear their abjuration oath, should be drowned. It would still be true that two women in humble life—one harmless from age, and the other from youth—were sentenced, under that law, to die that death, and must have been immediately executed had the Government's instructions been followed out; and that it was only from the accidental circumstance that the Commissioners happened to be more humane than those who appointed them, that the execution of the sentence was deferred. It would still be true that, when the Government had again the case of these women before them, though knowing their repugnance to the abjuration oath, they still made their swearing it the condition of their escaping the death to which they had been doomed,—thus inflicting, it may be, a severer suffering even than death. Little, in truth, can the 'Crown' gain, even were Mr. Napier to gain his 'Case.' He may affix a stigma on the Church of Scotland, and deprive her martyrs of the honour that has been paid to their memory; but he will not remove from the Restoration Government the deep reproach that impartial history must record against it, nor free the Episcopal Church in Scotland of that day from the dishonour of inciting to the cruelties of these times.

C

CHAPTER II.

MR. NAPIER'S PROOF ON THE NEGATIVE SIDE EXAMINED, AND
SHOWN TO BE INCONCLUSIVE.

IT is admitted by Mr. Napier that, on the 27th March 1685, a Royal
Commission of Justiciary, for the southern and western districts,
was appointed by the Privy Council, under the presidency of the Prime
Minister's brother, Colonel James Douglas. It is admitted that 'one
of the special instructions under which he acted, and which had been
issued at the close of the year 1684, for the direction of all Royal
Commissioners, was,' that men who were found guilty of owning or
not disowning the principles of Renwick's Proclamation, were 'to be
hanged immediately in the place;' and that women, in like manner
found guilty, were 'to be drowned.'[1] It is admitted further, that
while this Commission was sitting at Wigtown, the two women,
Margaret Lauchlison and Margaret Wilson, were tried and condemned.
'While Douglas's Commission was sitting at Wigtown,' says Mr.
Napier, 'two women; and *only two*, were tried, and condemned to
death.'[2] Thus, while admitting that a capital sentence was passed
on *two* women, he denies the trial and condemnation of Margaret
Wilson's younger sister, Agnes, of whom Wodrow, on the authority
of the Penninghame Session minute, affirms that she was tried and
condemned at the same time, but that she was released, on her father
giving a bond of £100 sterling to produce her when called.

The story of Agnes Wilson, though given by Wodrow on the
authority of the session of the parish in which she lived, is denied
by Mr. Napier on these grounds: 1*st*, She was said to be only *thirteen*
years of age, and the Commission had no authority to try any who
were not *above the age of sixteen*; 2*d*, 'If condemned to death along
with her adult sister, would she not have been reprieved along with
her? Do we require further evidence to satisfy us that *that* part of
Wodrow's story at least is a falsehood,—as absurd as it is calumnious?
Are we bound to be tender of it, and to give it a gentler name?'[3]
He argues, too, that the 'domestic history of the family of the
Wilsons,' as given by Wodrow, is 'incredible'—a moral impossibility,
contrary to human nature and common sense. 'Are we to believe

---

[1] *Case for the Crown*, p. 26.   [2] *Ibid.*, p. 28.   [3] *Ibid.*, p. 13.

that a girl of eighteen, taking along with her, from the nursery of her Episcopalian parents, a sister of thirteen and a brother of sixteen, all with their infantine minds devoted to martyrdom, and sternly made up to the Presbyterian *dogma* and battle-word, that "Christ alone is King and Head of his Church" (meaning none but their own form of a church), rushed from their well-conditioned home, "fled, and lived in the wild mountains, bogs, and caves" (which harboured the assassins of Archbishop Sharp, and the midnight murderers of the good minister of Carsphairn), until brought back by the violent exertions of an Executive, deeply occupied at the time watching Argyle's invasion, to dungeons, and martyrdom, or murder; the *loyal* Episcopalian parents being, at the same time, robbed by Government of all their great plenishing, and consigned to utter ruin? Are we to believe all that story, in the face of human nature—in the face of common sense? . . . . . And what are we to say of the minister and Kirk-Session of Penninghame, who gathered, prepared, recorded, attested, and sealed with prayer, the most abominable nonsense that ever outraged the truth and justice of history?'[1]

Our previous chapter was designed as a general answer to such arguments as the above, oft repeated in the *Case for the Crown*, viz. that whatever seems at variance with human nature and common sense, must not be believed if imputed to the Restoration Governments. The instructions given to the Commissioners sent to Livingstone and the adjoining parishes, will probably now come to the reader's recollection. They were to 'make prisoners of all persons *above the age of twelve years*,' in the families of those who might be executed, 'in order to transplantation.' The Government which could resolve to banish and sell as slaves children above twelve years, *who had committed no crime*, may be supposed capable of apprehending and prosecuting a child of thirteen years who was a transgressor. Mr. Napier mentions a case from the Privy Council records (23d January 1679), to show that those so young were not subjected to punishment. The Council ordered the magistrates of Leith to set at liberty 'James Lawson, a boy of about the age of fourteen years, prisoner there upon account of conventicles.' It may be true, as Mr. Napier says, that the 'Council ordered his release on account of his youth,' but still it is manifest that he was apprehended, tried, and condemned to punishment, *notwithstanding his youth*. The Council records might furnish Mr. Napier with a still more remarkable case of youthful transgression and Privy Council humanity. There is laid before them, on 19th May 1685, a petition from Patrick Maxwell of Tilline, aged *eleven*, 'incarcerat in Dundee' with his mother on a charge of 'being present with her at field preachings and house conventicles.' We do not wonder that this small child was let out of jail when he petitioned, but we do wonder that he was 'incarcerat,' for that implies apprehension and presumed guilt. After this, there is nothing incredible in Agnes Wilson's case.

[1] *Case for the Crown*, pp. 121, 122.

She was older, and doubtless a worse offender. She went to conventicles too; but not, like this little boy, at her mother's apron-string. She went contrary to parental example and counsel, and was consequently looked on as a great transgressor. So say the Penninghame Session, and Wodrow after them; but others, besides Mr. Napier, may ask (probably in politer terms), Can we believe them?

We shall endeavour, in the proper place, to show on what grounds the Kirk-Session of Penninghame are to be accounted trustworthy as regards the whole family history of the Wilsons; but, in the meantime, we shall produce a witness against whom Mr. Napier will not have so violent a prejudice as against the Presbyterian minister and his session,—that witness being Mr. James Colhoun, the Episcopal minister of Penninghame from 1666 to 1689, and therefore at the time when the events in dispute occurred. An exact copy of Mr. Colhoun's list of parishioners above twelve years of age, as given in to the authorities, is now before us, dated 29th September 1684; and neither Margaret Wilson, nor Thomas, nor Agnes, are entered in the list as residing with their parents at Glenvernock, but, as has been already stated, they all appear (even Agnes) in the appended list of withdrawers from worship, and are described as 'somtyme in Glenvernock,' showing that they were not there at the time the list was drawn up. This proves that they had 'rushed from their well-conditioned home,' and 'fled,' and had betaken themselves to the mountain caves. Whither but to such retreats could they have gone? for when their parents could not harbour them, who else would run that risk? So far, then, this family history is *proved*; and the fact that *Agnes*, as well as Margaret, was in Mr. Colhoun's black list, accounts for her apprehension and trial along with her sister. Mr. Napier may explain, as he best can, how 'an Executive deeply occupied at the time watching Argyle's invasion' should have wasted their energies in capturing and trying young girls; and may reconcile, if he can, that policy with 'human nature' and 'common sense;' for that such was their policy, cannot now be disputed.

The tendering of an oath to one so young as Agnes Wilson is at least as easily explained as the undoubted fact, that one so young was accused to the authorities; and it is certainly a more probable explanation of this difficulty to conceive that Royal Commissioners might, in this instance, have exceeded their instructions, or even made a mistake as to the age of the girl in question, than that a kirk-session, who had perfect knowledge of the facts of the case, should have recorded, and sent forth for immediate publication, a wilful and easily detected falsehood.

As to the other objection, that had Agnes Wilson been tried and condemned with her sister she must also have been respited along with her, *that* is sufficiently answered by the statement, that her father obtained her release by granting a bond for her production when required; which bond was forfeited. Probably, too, the error the Commissioners had fallen into regarding her age, may have rendered her release the more easily obtained. Nor is there anything 'incredible' in that part of the family history of the Wilsons, that the father of this family, though he conformed to the Established worship himself, was fined, and well-nigh ruined, for his children's transgressions of the church laws; for were not parents bound for the fines incurred by their children? and were they not obliged to give bonds for their payment?[1] Was not this a matter to which Claverhouse had pledged himself to Queensberry, the head of the Government, to give his special attention,—the head of the family living regularly himself, and allowing the female members of his family to run wild in transgression? The Sheriff of Galloway 'resolved' that 'the jest shall pass no longer here;' and Mr. Napier will not say that his hero made such resolves, and could not carry them out. He could both resolve and *do* things more bold and more cruel than drive off the cattle of Gilbert Wilson of Glenvernock. Nor must we forget the fact, of which Mr. Colhoun has put us in possession, that Gilbert Wilson was constrained to drive his children from their home. They were forced to flee to the mountains, just because he could no longer harbour them. How much he must have suffered, in the shape of fining and military quartering, before he was brought to obey the command to forbid his three children—his whole family—the shelter of his roof, those acquainted with ' human nature' will best understand.

Mr. Napier's strong denial of Wodrow's *History*, and his rather too energetic repudiation of Wodrow's authorities, so far as they relate to the story of Agnes Wilson, has led to this necessary digression from the case of the two principal sufferers, whose trial and death-sentence he admits. We now return to the main subject of his argument.

The petition on behalf of the elder of the two women, recently found in the Register House, Edinburgh, shows the date of their trial and condemnation to have been the 13th April 1685. The accusation brought against them, according to the Penninghame Session minute, was rebellion, and attending field and house conventicles; and, according to the petition above mentioned, *not disowning* 'the Apologetical Declaration' (Renwick's), and 'refusing the oath of abjuration of the same.' It is not likely that either of the women had ever borne arms against the Government, so that part of their accusation could not have been proved. That they attended conventicles, or the preaching of the ejected ministers, was doubtless true, and was probably owned and gloried in by them; and it is likely equally true that they refused to take an oath which, whatever may be its true import, *they considered* as a solemn disavowal of all sympathy with those of every shade of opinion who opposed the arbitrary proceedings of the Government, and a solemn pledge that they would renounce their own form of worship, and conform to another of which they disapproved. Mr. Napier says, that however

[1] See ' Proclamation of Council with Bond,' quoted Wodrow, vol. ii. p. 364.

' violent in their treason they might have been before,' had ' they at
their trial submitted to take the abjuration oath,' they would have
been ' liberated.'[1]   It is admitted, then, that they would not, at their
trial, take the abjuration, and that this refusal was really the ground
of their capital sentence.   It is admitted that they had resolution
enough to hear their doom of death pronounced, when they might
have saved their lives by merely taking the oath tendered to them.
' They must have been very *obstinate* at their trial,' says Mr. Napier;
but others will probably say that mere obstinacy will not satisfactorily
explain this moral phenomenon.   Most people will think that that
sacred thing *conscience* affords a better explanation; and even those
who think that their consciences must have been very unenlightened,
may see that they accepted their sentence of death *rather than do
what they believed to be wrong.*

Mr. Napier gives credit to the Royal Commissioners for their
clemency, inasmuch as ' the women were not ordered for immediate
execution on the place, as the instructions of the Privy Council
warranted'—he should have said ' required.'   Very likely the Commissioners were annoyed by the ' obstinacy' of their female criminals,
who would not take their oath, thus rendering a sentence of death a
necessity, unless this famous law against women was to become at
once null and void.   It is easy to conceive, without ascribing to the
Commissioners either much wisdom or much clemency, that they
must have seen that it would be well if the execution of their sentence could be dispensed with.   It was all very well for them to
frighten women into compliance with the wishes of the Government
by the terrors of being drowned.   But when a case like this occurred,
—when two women, one very old, and the other very young, resolutely
refused their oath, and stood firmly to hear sentence of death passed
on them,—it is no wonder that the Commissioners hesitated to carry
out a sentence which, they could not but see, would bring odium
upon their cause, and that they departed from their instructions so far
as not to order them for ' immediate' execution, doubtless hoping that
their ' obstinacy' would give way, and that they would be brought to
comply with the terms of the Government, and petition for a reversal
of their sentence.   Now that they were condemned, the Commissioners could do no more than allow them time to petition for royal
clemency.   They could not reverse their own sentence; nor could the
Privy Council.   King James in London alone could do so, and doubtless he would exercise his prerogative, if recommended to do so by the
Council.

Thus far, those on both sides of the question at issue are agreed as
to the facts of the case, so far as they relate to the two principal prisoners.   But from this point difference begins.   Mr. Napier says that
the two women did petition the Privy Council for their lives, owning
the justice of their sentence, and promising to take the abjuration, and
conform to Episcopal worship; that they were removed to Edinburgh

[1] *Case for the Crown*, p. 29.

before the 30th April, and, at that date, reprieved by the Privy Council to another date left blank ; that they were recommended to the King for pardon, and were *actually pardoned and liberated*.

But how much of this has Mr. Napier actually proved ? *First*, Did the two women petition the Government? There was lately found in the Register House, Edinburgh, the original petition of Margaret Lauchlison to the Privy Council, authenticated, but not in a very satisfactory way, by William Moir, notary-public, the petitioner herself being unable to write.[1] No petition from Margaret Wilson has been found ; but the fact of her being included in the reprieve of the Privy Council affords reasonable grounds to believe that she had also petitioned, *or been petitioned for*, in similar terms.

No one, however, can assuredly affirm that these petitions *expressed the sentiments of the two women, or that it was with their concurrence and approval that petitions expressed in such terms were sent to the Government.* At their trial they resolutely refused the Government oath, and allowed sentence of death to be recorded against them, when they had every reason to expect that they would be sent to immediate execution, in terms of the law under which they were tried. It is not easy to believe, that no sooner were they relieved from the fear of immediate death than they owned the justice of their sentence, and offered to comply with all the Government asked them to do.

The petition which has been found is evidently not the petition of the illiterate old woman as regards its *style ;* and it may be supposed

---

[1] ' Unto his Grace my Lord High Commissioner, and remanent Lords of his Majesties Most Honourable Privie Counsell ;

' The humble supplication of Margaret Lachlisone, and now prisoner in the Tolbuith of Wigton—

' Sheweth:

' That whereas I being justlie condemned to die, by the Lords Commissioners of his Majesties Most Honourable Privie Counsell and Justiciore, in ane Court holden at Wigtoune, the threttein day of Apryle *instant,* for my not disowning that traiterous apollogetical declaration laitlie affixed at severall paroch churches within this kingdom, and my refusing the oath of abjuration of the saymein, which was occasioned by my not perusing the saymein : And now, I having considered the said declaratione, doe acknowledge the saymein to be traiterous, and tends to nothing but rebellione and seditione, and to be quyt contrair unto the wrytin word of God ; and am content to abjure the same with my whole heart and soull:

' May it therefoir please your Gràce, and remanent Lords as said is, to take my cais to your serious consideratione, being about the age of thre-scor ten years, and to take pitie and compassione on me, and recall the foirsaid sentence so justlie pronouncet against me; and to grant warrant to any your Grace thinks fit to administrat the oath of abjuration to me, and upon my taking of it to order my liberatione; and your supplicant shall leive, heirafter ane good and faithful subject in tyme cuming; and shall frequent the ordinances and live regularly, and give what other obedience your Grace and remanent Lords sall prescryve thereanent; and your petitioner shall ever pray.

' De mandato dictæ Margaretæ Lauchlisone scribere nescien, ut asseruit, ego Gulielmus Moir, notarius-publicus, subscribo testante hoc meo chyrographo.

' J. Dunboir, *witness*.

' Will. Gordoun, *witness*.'

that it is as little her's as regards its *matter* and *substance*. The friendly hand that drew it framed it to suit the views of the Government, and to obtain their pardon, in the hope that the old woman would succumb, and accept of her life on the terms on which alone she could be pardoned.[1]

With regard to Margaret Wilson, too, it may well be believed that any petition in her favour was the work of her friends, and that she never consented to renounce by solemn oath those principles, for her stedfast adherence to which she had been condemned. This accords with the statement, that in prison she wrote 'a vindication of her refusing to save her life by taking the abjuration, and engaging to conformity.'[2] Her writing such a vindication implied efforts made on her behalf, but without her consent; efforts that might have been successful had she consented to the terms. The most natural and probable theory is, that both women were petitioned for by their friends in the hope that, should the Government give a favourable answer, they might be brought to comply so far with the demands of the Government, that their lives would be spared. That they who, in the awe-inspiring presence of a court of justice, could firmly hear their death-sentence rather than take the oath tendered to them, should immediately thereafter recant their creed in the abject terms that Mr. William Moir puts into the mouth of the elder prisoner, is neither natural nor probable.

Secondly, Has Mr. Napier proved that the two women were removed to Edinburgh before the 30th April, and at that date reprieved by the Privy Council *sine die ?* There is no doubt that the petitions in favour of the two women obtained for them on the 30th April a reprieve by the Privy Council in the form subjoined.[3] The existence of this reprieve is no recent discovery. Wodrow states that he had seen it, and gives it as *his opinion* that 'the people at Wigtown (he means those who acted for the Government there) 'were deeply guilty,

---

[1] It may be said that William Moir, being an officer sworn to do his duty faithfully, could not have subscribed any petition that was not *bona fide* the petition of the prisoner. No doubt he had her authority to draw out a petition to the Government for her life, but it need not be supposed that she dictated its terms; and it is a remarkable circumstance that it does not appear from the docquet that the petition was read to the old woman, or even subscribed in her presence.

[2] Wodrow, iv. 248.

[3] 'The Lords of his Majesty's Privy Council doe hereby reprive the execution of the sentance of death pronounced by the Justices against Margaret Wilson and Margaret Lauchlison untill the   day of   ; and discharges the Magistrates of Edinburgh for putting of the said sentence to execution against them, untill the forsaid day: and recommends the said Margaret Wilson and Margaret Lauchlison to the Lords Secretaries of State to interpose with his most sacred Majesty for the royal remission of them.' At this sederunt of the Privy Council there were present—'His Majesty's High Commissioner (Queensberry), the Lord Chancellor, Atholl, Drumlanrig, Strathmore, Southesque, Panmuir, Tweedale, Balcarres, Kintore, Viscount Tarbat, Livingstoun, Kinnaird, President of Session, The Advocate (Sir Geo. Mackenzie), Justice-Clerk, Castlehill, Sir George Monro, Gosfoord.'

and had no power for what they did.' In this opinion he may be right, or he may be wrong; but at all events the circumstance of a reprieve having been granted was enough to give rise to the tradition which has always prevailed,—that there was something illegal in the execution. The history of the execution given by Wodrow, on the authority of the Penninghame Session minute, *implies that there was a reprieve*, and that the Government officials at Wigtown had power to spare the lives of the prisoners, on their taking the abjuration. When some of Margaret Wilson's friends, after she was in the water, represented to Major Winram that she had complied, or was willing to comply, with the Government test, ' the Major came near and offered her the abjuration, charging her instantly to swear it, otherwise to return to the water. Most deliberately she refused, and said, " I will not." ' If the Privy Council, on being petitioned, had not returned a favourable reply in the form of a reprieve, Major Winram could not have offered the abjuration as a means of still escaping death. That he did so, clearly shows that he had instructions from the Council to that effect. Whether he had instructions to execute the sentence of the Commissioners in the event of the prisoners refusing the abjuration, cannot now be ascertained.

That the date to which the reprieve extended was left blank, is a remarkable circumstance. It was evidently so framed to suit contingencies,—to allow time for a royal pardon to be got, should the abjuration be taken; and perhaps *to allow the sentence of the Commissioners at once to take effect, should the oath be refused;* for it may be that the Government was informed that these criminals were not quite so ready to take the oath, as the petitions in their favour made them declare.

But then it is not any one at Wigtown, but most distinctly *the Magistrates of Edinburgh*, who are discharged from executing the sentence in question. On this circumstance Mr. Napier builds his theory, that the two women (who, it will be kept in mind, were condemned on the 13th April, and who thereafter, at a date not given, petitioned the Privy Council from the Tolbooth of Wigtown) were taken to Edinburgh, and had taken the abjuration *there* prior to the 30th April, the date of their reprieve. Is it a likely thing that the Royal Commissioners, who had already transgressed their instructions by not carrying out their sentence 'immediately at the place,' took it upon themselves to send to Edinburgh those whom they had condemned to be drowned at Wigtown, as if assured that the Government would reverse their sentence? The sentence doubtless was, that they were to be executed *at Wigtown by drowning.* Neither the Royal Commissioners, nor any other official of the Government, would dare to remove the women from the place where they were, according to their sentence, to be executed, till the deliverance of the Privy Council on their petition was known.

And surely it was not necessary to send them to Edinburgh to have the abjuration administered to them *there.* The petition in

favour of the elder woman craves the High Commissioner, and remanent Lords of the Council, ' to grant warrant *to any your Grace thinks
fit* to administrat the oath of abjuration to me, and upon my taking it,
to order my liberation.' The natural course to be followed, in the
circumstances, was just to grant warrant to some of their officials at
Wigtown to administer the oath ; and thereafter, it may be, to send
them to Edinburgh to await the pleasure of the King, who alone could
grant a pardon. And if it was the instruction of the Council, that,
after being sworn, they should be sent to headquarters, this will explain
why it was that the Magistrates of Edinburgh, into whose custody
they would in that case be given, were discharged from executing
their sentence. On the supposition that no such instruction was
given, the word 'Edinburgh' in the reprieve may be regarded as a
clerical error of the not very accurate scribe, who, in the same register,
and about the same time, when dealing with a similar case of life and
death, wrote, 'James Meason, tailior, Ochiltree,' instead of 'James
Napper, mason, Ochiltree,'[1]—thus reprieving a mythical personage not
much in danger of being *hanged*, and leaving the *real man*, towards
whom the Council had merciful intentions, still under sentence of death.

We are of opinion, however, that there is no necessity for supposing that there is a clerical error in the Council minute. It appears
to have been the general rule followed by the Council, to order those
who were capitally convicted, but whom they were willing to recommend to mercy, to be brought to Edinburgh, there to await further
proceedings in their case. This was done, probably because it would
have been too great a letting down of the majesty of the law to sentence people to be executed, and then, on their calling out *peccavimus*,
and taking an oath, to set them free, in the sight of those who had
seen them solemnly condemned. Hence an order for removal to
Edinburgh, and a considerable delay, was apparently the Government's
method, in cases where a reprieve was granted and a recommendation
for pardon contemplated. In the Wigtown case, it is probable that
the Council, presuming that the women would comply with their
terms, ordered them to be forwarded to Edinburgh, and framed their
minute *proleptically*, committing them to the keeping of the Magistrates of Edinburgh as prisoners under sentence, but respited. Such
a minute (and it must be remarked that this is the only minute
regarding these women in the Council records) would serve at once as
a warrant for their removal from the Tolbooth of Wigtown, and for
their reception and detention in that of Edinburgh.

[1] *Case for the Crown*, note, p. 38. This, it will be shown below, was not the only
blunder in the minutes relating to James Napper and other two men condemned at
Cumnock. One minute regarding them seems to have been quite forgotten by the
Council and their clerk ; and when, passing over it, they refer to an earlier one, they
mis-state the duration of their reprieve, writing *June* instead of May.

In the Council Register, too, such entries as the following occur : ' 4 *July* 1685.—Mr.
George Meldrum of Crombie, prisoner in *the Tolbooth of Edinburgh.*' 'Tolbooth of
Edinburgh' is then erased, and 'Castle of Blackness' interlined above.

If we suppose that, on the reception of this minute by the Government officials at Wigtown, the women refused the oath as resolutely as they had done at their trial (which is in itself a probable supposition, and which our proof, to be hereafter adduced, will show was actually the case), then, in these circumstances, their removal to Edinburgh would never be thought of. That was a thing not easily done at the time, and would not be done needlessly.

It may have been, that along with the reprieve the Council forwarded instructions to Major Winram and the other officials appointed to administer the oath, how they were to act if the oath should still be refused. But if the Council had no *private* information, but acted on such information merely as Mr. Moir's petition conveyed, it is probable that they anticipated no refusal of the oath, and gave no instructions to meet that contingency. In that case the officials at Wigtown would be left to their own discretion; and if, in such circumstances, they took away life, it is easy to conceive that their doing so would be regarded by some as a wanton and lawless act, and thus the idea would gain prevalence among those who did not know all the facts of the case, that the execution took place without a legal sentence.

On the supposition that the prisoners would not take the oath, and that the Government officials had no special instructions how to act should that be the case, it is clear that only one or other of two courses of proceeding lay open to them. They might delay further proceedings till they had consulted with the Government; or they might take it upon themselves to anticipate what would be the Government's deliverance in such circumstances, and resolve to carry out the sentence. From this latter course they would not be restrained by the fear of a pardon coming after the execution; for they would be perfectly certain that no pardon would be asked by the Council till the prisoners had taken the required oath. Nor yet would they be restrained by the fear of carrying severity beyond the mind of the Government; for at this very time (8th May) the Parliament were enacting a new penal statute, ordaining that 'such as shall be present, *as hearers*, at field conventicles shall be punished with DEATH, and confiscation of goods.'[1]

The resolution of the Government's Executive at Wigtown, to proceed to carry out the sentence of the Commissioners, would be taken all the more readily from their still imagining that, when the women saw that their execution was really resolved on if they would not swear the oath required, they would certainly comply, and so save their lives; while at the same time all onlookers would see that the law was not to be trifled with, and that the rulers were resolved to inflict the penalty of death on man or woman who would not abjure hostility to the Government.

That those who had charge of the execution still imagined that their prisoners would yield at last, when subjected to the ordeal

[1] Wodrow, vol. iv. p. 272.

by water, appears exceedingly probable, from the mode in which it is said the execution was proceeded with,—a mode probably not quite in accordance with the sentence of the Commissioners. In the absence of the record, we cannot of course say what the exact terms of the sentence were; but the sentence given in the Penninghame Session minute, and written in a large hand, as if it were a transcript, if not from a record, at least from some one's memory, we may suppose to be substantially that which was passed. The judges sentenced them 'to be tyed to palisados fixed in the sand, within the flood-mark, and there to stand till the flood overflowed them and drowned them.' Now, to carry out that sentence, we must suppose the women bound fast, in an upright posture, to stakes fixed in the sand, *and left to stand there alone*, to be gradually covered by the advancing tide. Evidently their executioners could not remain with them, or near them, without sharing their fate. This is the mode of execution which Shiels, in his work, *A Hind let Loose*, would lead us to think was adopted; and his frontispiece to that work represents two women tied back to back to one stake. Of course the artist[1] has given us a fancy picture; but an execution, according to Shiels' text, would have been according to what was probably the actual sentence. Now the Penninghame minute, while recording what was probably the sentence, gives a description of the execution not exactly in accordance therewith, while the account given in the Kirkinner minute is equally irreconcilable with it. This kirk-session says of the old woman, their parishioner, that she was 'fixed to the stake till the tide made, and held down within the water by one of the town officers, by his halbert at her throat, till she died.' The other session says of the young woman, that 'before her breath was quite gone they *pulled her up*, and held her till she could speak, and then asked her if she would pray for the King,' and when she refused, 'returned her into the water;' or, as Wodrow says, 'she was thrust down again into the water.' Mr. Napier naturally enough asks, How, if the women were firmly and closely tied to stakes, could all this be done 'with the tide of the Solway rushing overhead?'[2] The *manner* in which the drowning was accomplished became a matter of controversy in the beginning of the 18th century. An Episcopalian writer, whose important testimony will be quoted in our proof, and who, from his position, must have been thoroughly acquainted with all the circumstances connected with the execution, admits that the women were drowned, but denies emphatically that they were 'tyed to stakes within the flood-mark till the sea came up,' as represented in *A Hind let Loose*. He does not tell us how they were executed, but he denies that it was in the way there represented, and apparently commonly

[1] The *Hind let Loose* was almost certainly printed in Holland, and the frontispiece engraved there.

[2] *Case for the Crown*, p. 7. It will be remarked that neither of the session records speak of Margaret Wilson being 'unbound,' the word used by Lord Macaulay, and on which Mr. Napier runs riot.

believed. And why does he dispute this apparently small point ? He had an object in doing so ; and that, we conceive, was to free the authorities of the blame of executing their prisoners in a way that shut the door of mercy against them *at once*, whereas it was actually left open to them to the very last. This writer's information, though merely negative, is important, and prepares us to receive as true the mode of the execution described in a pamphlet entitled *Popery Reviving*, published in Edinburgh in 1714. The writer of this pamphlet, at page 26, gives the usual account of the two women, and of their trial and sentence, and then goes on to describe the manner of their death :—

'Some time after, the said sentence was thus executed. Two stups of timber were fastened upon the brink of the water of Blednoch (to which place the sea flows always at high water), and the prisoners are brought, under the guard of a troop of dragoons, commanded by Major Winram, to the place of execution ; and after being allowed some time to perform their last duties of devotion, which they did with so much Christian. calmness and sweet submission to the pleasure of Almighty God, and in such a lively dependence upon Him for salvation through Christ, that their behaviour extorted tears from some of the soldiers that guarded them, the manner of their execution was: Cords were tyed to the foresaid stups, and to their bodies, and they thrown over the brink of the river into the water and drowned. There is one thing finally to be taken notice of, that the old woman was first despatched, in order to terrify the young woman to a compliance with such demands and oaths as were required of her ; but the view of her fellow-sufferer's death did not in the least shake her stedfastness in her resolution to adhere to her principles to the very last.'

Those who know the locality will at once see that this description removes many misconceptions hitherto entertained regarding, and clears up all the obscurities that have hitherto rested on, the manner of the drowning; that it entirely obviates the difficulties felt by many, as stated by Mr. Napier; and that it explains and accounts for the strong language of the Episcopalian writer already alluded to, who, in replying, in 1703, to a controversial opponent, admits that the ' women were drowned indeed,' but denies, in the strongest language, that they ' were tied to stakes within flood-mark till the sea came.' It is, too, in perfect consistency with the kirk-session accounts, though at variance with the scene depicted in the frontispiece of the *Hind let Loose*. It may be remarked that, in recent times, the course of the Blednoch has been changed by embankments, designed to gain land from the sea. But the older inhabitants of Wigtown remember when the river's course was close along the base of the hill on which the town stands, and when the shipping (only small coasting sloops) lay in the river's channel, close under the north-east end of the town, near the church and churchyard. From that point the river took a bend seaward, and cut for itself a deep canal-like channel through the soft sand. At low water, the sea recedes for miles from the town, leaving a large extent of naked sand traversed by the Blednoch. When the sea flows, it rushes rapidly up the channel of the river, and then gradually overflows its banks on both sides; but near the town, where the execution is said to have taken place,[1] its advance is not so rapid, and it is easy to conceive the scene described in the above extract being there enacted. While the deep channel of the river (at that season of the year a tiny stream) was being filled up by the flowing tide, the executioners might stand on the bank, drive in their stubs or stakes, fasten their cords to them and to the persons of the prisoners, and force them over the bank, to stand till the deepening waters overwhelmed them. Those who thus carry out the sentence are themselves in no danger, and yet close at hand to stop the work of death, if there should be any sign of failing resolution. They can, without any unbinding of cords or unloosening of knots, 'pull up' the penitent, upon the first cry indicating a change of mind. But still, the time allowed cannot be long; 'the tide of the terrible Solway' will not wait, but will soon overflow the bank, and drive the executioners from their firm footing on the sand. So they can hardly wait for the tide doing its work. They hasten death, in the case of the elder sufferer, by forcibly holding her down with a halbert under the water, in the hope still to save the life of the younger, by awing her into submission at the sight of the death-struggle of her aged friend. But she remains firm, and refuses the 'sinful oath.' The rushing tide soon overwhelms her also, and the tragedy ends.

If we suppose that the presiding official led forth the two prisoners to the sands of the bay of Wigtown, in the confident expectation that their 'obstinacy' would give way *at the last*, when they saw death close at hand, and that thus the merciful designs of the Government would be accomplished, and the authority of the law maintained in the view of the attending multitude, who would thus witness an edifying recantation of rebellious principles, it is easy to see that, having entered on this course, he must needs go on to extremities should there be no recantation. He could not, in such circumstances, stop short in the middle of the execution, without making such an exhibition of the feebleness of the law as would render it utterly contemptible in the eyes of the people. And while he thus thought of the multitude before him, he doubtless also thought of his masters at headquarters, and took into account what they would think of his conduct, were he to make void one of their penal laws, at the very time when they were enacting a new one.

It must not be imagined that we are assuming as a fact *that* which has to be proved. We are merely stating the case *hypothetically*. Supposing the execution to be a fact, we are attempting to show how it may be reconciled with the other undoubted fact of a reprieve granted on petitions in favour of the prisoners. A reprieve usually ends in a pardon, but not necessarily. Had we no evidence that there was an execution, we would assume it as possible, but not certain, that the reprieve was followed by a pardon; but if we have satisfactory proof that the execution took place, then we must explain,

---

[1] The spot pointed out by tradition as the scene of the drowning is now, by embankments, being turned into dry land.

as we best can, how the reprieve did not terminate as reprieves usually do.

The great point in the case on the negative side is the fact, that the reprieve discharges the Magistrates of Edinburgh from executing the prisoners; whence it is inferred that they were taken to Edinburgh, and consequently were not drowned at Wigtown. But may not the proof of the drowning be so strong that it would be impossible to resist it, even if it were proved that the removal to Edinburgh took place? These two facts are both *possible;* the one is not destructive of the other. But certainly it must be allowed that both are not *probable;* so if we find ground to believe that there was an execution, we shall be led to account for the term *Edinburgh* in the Council minute, in one or other of the ways above suggested; either as a *clerical error,* or, as we think more probable, an order of committal to Edinburgh, given in anticipation of the women's removal thither.[1]

Excepting the occurrence of the word *Edinburgh* in their reprieve, there is no proof whatever that the women were removed from Wigtown. Mr. Napier, indeed, gives a full account of the case of three Cumnock men—Allan Aitken, John Pearson, and James Napper —who had been condemned to death under the same Commission of Justiciary (for 'concealing and not revealing of these rebels who lately went through some western shires'), and who, on petitioning the Council, were reprieved, then removed to Edinburgh, and, after considerable delay, pardoned. This case is a most instructive one, as illustrative of the procedure of the Privy Council; and Mr. Napier deserves special thanks for fully reporting it, seeing it not merely does not prove *his case,* but even furnishes a weighty argument on the other side, as we shall presently show. In the meantime, it is enough to observe, that the removal of the three men from Cumnock to Edinburgh is no proof that the two women were also taken thither from Wigtown, and affords no ground whatever for Mr. Napier's confident conclusion, 'that the whole of these petitioning convicts, men and women, were transmitted to headquarters under the same escort.'[2] With regard to the men, we have proof of their removal in accordance with what appears to have been the general rule of the Council in such cases. With regard to the women, the word *Edinburgh* in their reprieve may merely indicate the *intention* of the Council to have them brought to headquarters, but cannot be regarded as proof that they were actually brought, especially in the face of evidence to the contrary.

[1] The grounds for considering the term *Edinburgh* in the Council minute not a clerical error, but for regarding the minute as an order given to the Magistrates of Edinburgh in anticipation of the women's removal thither, are exceedingly well stated in a review of the first edition of this pamphlet in the *Scotsman* (8th August 1867). To the writer of that article, and of a subsequent one (4th September 1867), we tender special thanks, not only for giving our views a wide circulation, but for his contribution of *new materials* in the argument. He will best understand our appreciation of his services by the free use we make of his contributions.   [2] *Case for the Crown,* p. 40.

But whether the two women were taken, or ordered to be taken, to Edinburgh or not, it may be thought that the fact of a reprieve being granted, and a recommendation to the Crown for a pardon being agreed to by the Privy Council, is proof that, before the date of their reprieve, they must have taken the abjuration. Would the Council reprieve, and recommend to be pardoned, persons who had not yet abjured those treasonable principles, for not disowning which they had been condemned? To this it may be answered, that if the Council did at all entertain the petitions forwarded to them on behalf of the two prisoners at Wigtown, craving that they might be allowed to take the abjuration, with a view to the remission of their sentence, *the deliverance of the Council must have been in the form of a reprieve.* No one could administer the abjuration to prisoners under sentence, without the authority of the Council; and the granting of such authority by the Council was in fact a reprieve. It implied that the Council were willing to spare their lives, if the oath were taken. At the same time, the defective form of the reprieve showed that the Council were sufficiently wary. Such a reprieve was no bar to the execution of the sentence, if the prisoners did not comply with the terms on which their lives were offered to them.

That the Council did grant reprieves, on the petition of convicts, *prior to their taking the oath, and while they were still at the place where they had been condemned,* is proved by the case of the Cumnock men. These three men, who were sentenced to be hanged on the 20th April (of course at Cumnock, where sentence was passed on them), had their case brought before the Council on the 9th April, by 'ane address,' in which they 'acknowledge their great ignorance, error, and fault, and cast themselves upon the King's mercy, and are content to take any oaths or obligations by law appointed.' 'Which address being read in the Council, the Lord Commissioner, his Grace, hath reprieved, and hereby reprieveth, the execution of the foresaid sentence of death until the twentieth day of May next, at which time the same to be put in execution, in caise there be no furder order to the contrairie.' Thus it seems that the *first movement* of the Council in the way of mercy was in the form of a reprieve. This, we may infer, was the way in which they granted authority to administer the oath, and thereafter to send the convicts to Edinburgh, though the minute contains no instructions to that effect; for the next entry concerning these prisoners shows that both these things had been done,— that the oath had been administered, and the transmission taken place.

On the 8th May we find that these men, 'now prisoners in Tolbooth of Canongate,' again petition the Council, and are reprieved 'till furder order;' and the Council ordains a letter to be writ in their favours to the Lords Secretaries of State, recommending them to apply to the King for their pardon, 'in regard that they have taken the oath of abjuration,' etc. Mr. Napier, without proof, and contrary to probability, concludes that, being taken to Edinburgh, they 'had *there* taken the abjuration oath.' It is surely more likely that they took the oath *before* they were removed from the place where their execution was appointed. Their removal *at that time* was a matter of some trouble and difficulty, and we cannot imagine that this was done until the oath on which their pardon depended had been taken. But, be this as it may, it is of importance to notice, that though the Council, by this minute of the 8th of May, ordained a letter to be written to London in favour of these convicts, *no letter was then written.* The Council were not *prompt* in forwarding recommendations to mercy. Indeed, in this case, they seem to have forgotten the men, and their merciful intentions regarding them, till their memory is refreshed by another 'address' presented on the 5th of June.

The Council, on the 5th of June (having just passed through the tribulation occasioned by Argyle's invasion), seem to have had no recollection of what they had done in this Cumnock case on the 8th of May, and refer to their previous minute of the 9th of April, regarding which, too, their memory seems to have been at fault, for they state that the petitioners were then reprieved ' to the 20th day of June instant,' the fact being that the reprieve extended only to the 20th May. Now, however, their reprieve is extended till the 'first Friday of December,' and the Magistrates of Edinburgh are discharged, in the meantime, to put the sentence into execution. Again, the Council 'ordains a letter to be writt' to the Secretaries of State—the best possible proof that none was written when first 'ordained'—recommending them to mercy, ' in regaird they have sworn and subscribed the oath of the test.' Now, the letter to the Secretaries in London is written, *and the Council minute contains a copy of it.*

The Council minute of the last day of June 1685 shows satisfactorily how this Cumnock case ended, his Majesty's pardon being then 'produced by the Lord Chancellor.'

Here, then, is a case in which a petition for mercy, and an offer to take the Government oaths, ended in a pardon; and the minutes of the Privy Council show the steps by which it went on to this termination. But these minutes show that the Wigtown case, though it had a beginning, had no continuation, and had no such ending. It stopped short, from some cause, at the first stage,—at the mere permission to administer the oath, and forward the prisoners. No proof do these minutes furnish that the oath was administered, as in the case of the Cumnock men; no proof, deserving the name, that the women were actually sent to Edinburgh; no proof that a recommendation to mercy was actually forwarded to London; and, above all, *no proof that a pardon came.* It is possible to conceive some things done, in such a case, that are not recorded in the Acts of the Privy Council; but we cannot believe that prisoners condemned to death were liberated, on a royal pardon being received by the Council, without an entry to that effect appearing in their minutes, just as in the Cumnock case. In short, this Cumnock case, which Mr. Napier has so obligingly reported, *goes a far way to disprove his own case.*

We have not been informed whether or not Mr. Napier has had a.

D

search made in the State Paper Office, London, to ascertain if the links of proof, which are not to be found in Edinburgh, can be found *there*. If the case in question was sent to London, and the King's pardon obtained, official documents still extant in London relative to King James's Government of Scotland might be expected to furnish evidence that such is the fact. If Mr. Napier could say that, Though no pardon has been found in the Edinburgh records, here it is among the Government papers of the day, still preserved in the State Paper Office (one of several other acts of royal clemency), this would be the best point in his *Case for the Crown*, and it would give us on the other side some trouble to explain, how the pardon, actually granted, had miscarried. Mr. Napier may have left this promising field of evidence unexplored; though the friendly aid of certain London journalists who adopted his theory (we think on too slender grounds) might, we should imagine, have been engaged, without difficulty, on behalf of that side of the case which they had made their own. We conclude, however, that no search has been made that has led to the discovery of new evidence in the case, or we should have heard of it before now, and the *promised* new edition of the *Case for the Crown* would not have been so long in making its appearance.

But, whether or not the State Paper Office has been searched by those whose part it is to show that the pardon, which they say came from London to Edinburgh, was ever really granted in the former city, *we* are able to assure our readers that such a search has been made, and *made in vain*, for evidence to show that the Wigtown case was ever under consideration of the Crown with a view to pardon. Consequent upon the ventilation of Mr. Napier's theory, and of the support which it had received from a 'leading English journal of letters,' a gentleman of the legal profession, resident in London, was led, before adopting an opinion contrary to the hitherto received version of history, to examine the records of King James's Government, to see if there was *there* any evidence to show that a pardon had been granted to the Wigtown women. He has kindly communicated to us the *results* of his search, and sent us some valuable notes and extracts illustrative of those times. He has told us how the search was conducted by him, and permitted us to use his name to vouch for it.[1] His statement will show with what carefulness the search has been made, and it may serve to guide others who may wish further investigation. He says: 'The State Papers of the period relating to Scotland are contained in five large folio volumes, of 600 or 700 pages each. King James's warrants, and other communications with his Council and other authorities in Scotland, begin about the middle of the volume which is numbered IX., and run on to about 400 pages in the volume numbered XIII. Volumes IX. and X., which, you will see

[1] The gentleman who has thus kindly aided us in obtaining a truthful record of facts, and who deserves the thanks of the lovers of true history, both north and south of the Tweed, is Francis Turner, Esq., of the Middle Temple, and of the Home Circuit, barrister-at-law.

by the date, are most likely to have contained entries about the Wigtown women, I have turned over leaf by leaf, and have looked at, page by page. Volumes XI. and XII. I have examined by means of their very good indices, turning to any entry that seemed likely to bear upon the subject. Volume XIII. is not indexed, and I have therefore gone over that, entry by entry. The result is to satisfy me that no pardon was ever sent from London.'·

We have noticed the contrast presented by the Wigtown case and the Cumnock case, as they appear in the records of the Privy Council. The same contrast is still carried out in the London State Papers; for while the Wigtown case has not been found in them in any shape, in them may be found the Cumnock case, just as we might expect to find it, ending in the formal pardon, which, as it has never been before published, we subjoin in a note.[1]

But there is additional proof that Margaret Lauchlison and Margaret Wilson were never brought to Edinburgh. Supposing Mr. Napier's theory to be true, they must have been detained in some Edinburgh prison from the date of their reprieve, 30th April, till their pardon came. How long that would *probably* be, we may learn from the case of the Cumnock men. The Council first agreed to recommend *them* to mercy on the 8th May, and their pardon came on the 30th June, that is, in fifty-three days. But we know that the Council did not apply for their pardon when they promised to do so, but delayed writing till the 5th June. So we see that twenty-five days intervened between the Council's application and the receipt of the royal remission. Supposing, then, that the Wigtown case met with the same delay as the Cumnock one (and why should not the same cause retard both?), the two women must have continued prisoners in Edinburgh till about the 22d June. And even supposing that their letter of recommendation was forwarded to London on the 30th April, when it was

---

[1] Vol. x., No. 27, p. 32. Docquet of the Warrant for a Remission of Treason to Allan Aitken, John Pearson, and James Napper:—

'May it please your Majestie—

'These contain your Majesties Warrant (upon considerations above mentioned) for a Remission to passe your Majesties Exchequer and Great Seale of your ancient Kingdom of Scotland, to Allan Aitken in Cumnock, John Pearson, tailor there, and James Napper, mason in Ochiltree, for the Crime contained in the Processe and Doom of Fforfeiture, led and pronounced against them in a Justice Court holden within the Tolbooth of the Burgh of Cumnock, the third day of April last, by Colonell James Douglas, where they were convicted and found guilty of the Crime of Treason and Lese-Majesty, committed by them in concealing, and not revealing, the Rebells who went through some Western shires in armes some few days before, for which they were condemned to be executed to Death, and for the pain of Death therein contained ; and for all action and Crime following thereupon, or that may be imputed to them in their bodies only in time coming, Rehabilitating, Restoring, and Redintegrating them and their Heirs to their own names, good Names, Offices, and Privileges whereof they are deprived and prejudged by the said Fforfeiture, and also receiving and reponing them and their forsaids in and to your Majesties favor, mercy, and grace, ordaining these presents to passe through the Offices and Seales *gratis*, and declaring that this Remission shall no ways be extended to their

first agreed to, we might still expect (if their case met with just the same dispatch as the Cumnock one) to find them in an Edinburgh prison, at least till the 25th of May. *But we have proof that they were not in any Edinburgh prison even till the 18th of May.* Argyle's invasion, of which Mr. Napier makes so much use, comes in here to help our side of the case. The Earl's landing in the beginning of May cast the rulers in Edinburgh into a state of consternation. They forgot their designs of mercy towards the Cumnock men, as we have seen, and they probably forgot any similar intentions towards the Wigtown women. They seem, in fact, to have been afraid, not only of the rebels at large, but of the rebels in prison ; so they resolved to clear the jails of Edinburgh and Leith of ' all the prisoners for religion, especially those from the south and west,' and to send them northwards to Dunnottar.[1] This was done on the 18th of May. The prisoners were escorted down to Leith, and conveyed across the Firth to Burntisland, where a halt was made. Here orders were received from the Government to send back to Edinburgh such of the prisoners as would pledge themselves to loyalty by swearing the Government oaths ; and of the 134 men and 50 women then in bonds, 39 were *tested* and returned. The rest were marched on to their dreary captivity.

Now the point which claims attention is this. There are still preserved in the Register House, Edinburgh, among Privy Council warrants and other loose papers, *complete and formal lists of the prisoners* in the several jails of Edinburgh, Canongate, and Leith, and of those at Burntisland on the 20th May, and also of those who there took the oaths and were sent back to Edinburgh. In these lists we find many names with which Wodrow's history of previous years makes us familiar, and many Galloway names, too, which we met with in the record of the Commission at Wigtown in October 1684.

Lands, Heritages, Goods, or Gear belonging to them, the time of pronouncing the said sentence and Doom of Fforfeiture.

'Given at the Court at Whitehall the 25th day of June 1685, and of his Majesty's Reigne the first year.'

While the records of James's short reign contain not a few similar instances of Royal clemency shown to penitent and *submissive* rebels, they at the same time clearly show that the severe penal laws executed against those who would not pledge themselves, by oath, to implicit obedience to the tyranny of the times, had his Majesty's very cordial approval. Take the following as a specimen:—

Vol. x., No. 49, p. 59. King's Letter to the Secret Council *re* sueh obstinate Rebells as are to be transported to the Plantations.

'James R. [there follows the salutation]. Whereas, by your letter of the 30th day of July last past to our Secretaries, you propose that such of the Rebells, now prisoners, whom you think fit to be sent to our Plantations in America, and are so obstinate as that they will not own us or our authority, be stigmatized by having one of the ears of every one of them cut of : Wee have now thought fit to let you know that wee doe well approve of the same, and therefore doe hereby authorize and require you to take care that one of the ears of every such as aforesaid be cutt off before their being shipped in order to their transportation.'

[1] Wodrow, iv. 322.

Here, too, we find that even James Napper, John Pearson, and Allan Aitken, the three Cumnock men, who had before this time sworn the abjuration, and whom the Council had agreed to recommend to mercy, having, in the emergency of the times, given additional security for their good behaviour by swearing the test, were among the more fortunate ones who had a pleasure-trip to Burntisland and back. But we look in vain in these lists for the names of Margaret Lauchlison and Margaret Wilson. They were not among the prisoners who were cleared out on the 18th May. Their pardon, it may be said, might have been got from London in eighteen days. That is possible, but far from probable. The Government's motions in the direction of mercy were not so rapid in those days; while, if a pardon did come, the question still remains, What became of the women? where were they on the 18th–20th May? On no supposition could they, to use Mr. Napier's euphemism, have 'become expatriated' ere that time, for we know that the vessels employed in 'transplanting' the prisoners for religion did not sail till August. We may therefore conclude that the two women, not being prisoners in Edinburgh eighteen days after their case was, on 30th April, brought before the Council, were never prisoners there at any time.

The very defective evidence of the Privy Council records in favour of his side of the case, Mr. Napier endeavours to supplement from various quarters, and he seems to find 'corroborations' of his theory wherever he happens to look for them. In the Burgh records of Wigtown, he tells us, 'No trace of this martyrdom, nor of the names of the martyrs, is to be met with.' 'Considerable expense would have attended such a drowning scene as that described by fanatical romancers; and the fact that no single item indicating that any expense of the kind had been incurred by the Magistrates of Wigtown, amounts to excellent *negative* evidence that no such execution occurred there.'[1] It was very well to look into the Burgh records. There might have been some *incidental* notice of this case, just as there is in the records of the kirk-session; but no one is entitled to say that the absence of such notice goes to prove, in any way, that no such execution took place. It might afford slender evidence that the magistrates, as such, had nothing to do with the execution, as they had certainly nothing to do with the sentence. The Royal Commissioners, we know, had their own records; and the military in the district were placed under their command, and executed their sentences. They might have availed themselves of the services of the professional executioner of the place (and probably paid him), when one was to be found; and in those times such functionaries were not so scarce as they are now. For Mr. Napier, out of these Burgh records, brings to light a fact which, though it does not help to prove his case, at least illustrates the times. *The small burgh of Wigtown had a hangman of its own, at that very time receiving daily pay—'four shillings Scots daily.'* Even had it been the case that the magistrates

[1] *Case for the Crown*, pp. 44, 45.

had this duty imposed on them, it seems rather unreasonable in Mr. Napier not to believe in the execution, because he cannot find any account of the expense of it. For what did the hangman receive his daily wages but for doing such work when it was to be done ?

By the aid of his ' excellent negative evidence' Mr. Napier might indeed soon 'weed' out all Wodrow's martyrdoms, and clear the country of martyrs' monuments. He might even prove that Royal Commissioners were *myths*, as well as the martyrs; for he will find no proof of their existence in Burgh records. Even Queensberry and Claverhouse's great Commission in 1684, which did so much work and made so much stir, left no memorial of itself in the Burgh records of Wigtown; and we have undoubted authority for saying that no notice of it is found in those of Dumfries and Kirkcudbright, in each of which places it sat for two days, and, as we see from the records in the Register House, sentenced large numbers to punishment.

In short, the want of any proof that the Magistrates of Wigtown executed the sentence in question, in place of corroborating Mr. Napier's theory, just goes to confirm the kirk-session accounts; for they tell us, not that the magistrates, but that *Major Winram* was the presiding official at the execution; and if Wodrow represents *Provost Coltron* of Wigtown as an actor in the tragedy, he does so without the authority of the local church courts.[1]

But Mr. Napier's chief corroborative witness is Sir George Mackenzie, Lord Advocate during the reigns of Charles II. and James II. 'The last act,' says Mr. Napier, ' of his life, the last act of his able pen, was to vindicate himself, and the Government he had served so well, from the unscrupulous accusations of the anonymous pamphleteering Cameronians.' This *Vindication* was published in September 1691, four months after the death of Sir George; and this naturally gave rise to some suspicion of its genuineness. Granting,

---

[1] Mr. Napier endeavours to prove an *alibi* for the provost, and we think his proof on this point more satisfactory than his proofs generally are ; and as we see some think he has failed to establish even this point, we are glad to add a 'corroboration' to his proof of the provost's innocence. We learn from the old Wigtown session-book recently found, that when in 1704 Bailie M'Keand of Wigtown appeared before the kirk-session, to profess repentance for having 'sitten on the seize' when the two women were condemned to die, the provost was one of the members of session present. He, therefore, was most probably free from that scandal for which his brother magistrate was doing penance. Still, the fact that he was one of the three who undertook the odious task of tendering the *test* to the inhabitants of Wigtownshire in 1684, shows that he aided the Government in their measures, and his name is not much maligned by the tradition that hands him down as a persecutor. After the Revolution, he served in the kirk as an elder, attended the meetings of church courts, and watched over the morals of the people of Wigtown, taking his turn, week about with the other elders, in perambulating the town at a late hour, to see that all was orderly in the public-houses. But he does not seem to have kept so strict a watch upon himself as he should have done, for he was suspended from his functions as an elder for intemperance and profane swearing.

however, the testimony given in the *Vindication* to be really that
of the ex-Lord Advocate, even to the italics, it really is of little
weight. What does it say? 'There were indeed two women executed, and *but two*, in both these reigns; and they were punished
for most heinous crimes which no sex should defend.' These two,
it is allowed, were *Isobel Alison* and *Marion Harvey*, who were
hanged in the Grassmarket of Edinburgh in 1681, in the reign of
Charles II.; and it is left to be inferred that no female State prisoner
whatever suffered the last punishment of the law in the reign of
James II.

It must be kept in mind, that the *Vindication* was written in
answer to pamphlets on the other side, in which the Government was
accused of cruelty to women. The pamphlet, *A Hind let Loose*, was
published in 1687, four years before the *Vindication* was written by
Sir George; and was, doubtless, one of those accusations of his Government which he took up 'his able pen to answer.' And what does it
say on the subject of cruelty to the female sex? 'Neither were
women spared : some were hanged ; *some drowned tied to stakes within
the sea-mark*, to be devoured gradually with the growing waves, and
some of them very young, some of an old age.' In another pamphlet,
A Short Memorial of Sufferings and Grievances, etc., published in 1690,
the year before Sir George's death, occurs the following *item*, in the
catalogue of sufferings :—' The said Col. or Lieu.-Gen. James Douglas,
together with the laird of Lag, and Captain Winram, most illegally
condemned, and most inhumanly drowned, at stakes within the sea-
mark, two women at Wigtown, viz. Margaret Lauchlan, upwards of
sixty years, and Margaret Wilson, about twenty years of age, the foresaid fatal year 1685.' Of this pamphlet, Mr. Napier says, 'Doubtless,
Sir George Mackenzie, who died in London in the spring of 1691' (he
should have said the 8th of May), 'had never set eyes on that rubbish.' It is more than probable that one in Sir George's position,
writing in defence of the late Government, saw all the pamphlets, even
the most recent, that were written on the other side. But whether he
saw the *Memorial of Sufferings* or not, there is no doubt that he saw
A Hind let Loose, and the statement in it regarding the drowning of
women tied to stakes in the sea-mark; and he could not fail to observe that this was a reference to the Wigtown women who had been
reprieved at a meeting of the Privy Council at which he was present.
His Government was here plainly enough charged *with the drowning
of these two women*, for he knew that there was no other case of the
kind of which they could be accused. Why, then, did he not meet the
charge by a *direct denial?* Why did he not say then, as Mr. Napier
says now, 'A humane order had been issued by the Privy Council in
1685, that women, if condemned to death as traitors, were to suffer
simply by drowning, and neither to be hanged nor mangled, as might
happen to traitors of the other sex;[1] but though two women, and *but
two*, were sentenced to that death at Wigtown, they were not executed,

[1] *Case for the Crown*, p. 83.

but, on the contrary, were reprieved by the Privy Council and pardoned by the King ?' If Sir George Mackenzie could have made such a statement in vindication of his Government, would he not have made it ? Would he have left it to Mr. Napier to say, in 1863, what *he* could have said with much better effect in 1691 ? If he missed this point in his case, if it was in his brief, he was the most unskilful pleader that ever attained the high honour of being Lord Advocate of Scotland.

But it may be said that Sir George does deny the Wigtown execution, though in an *indirect* way. It would be better to say, he *ignores* it. He says nothing about it. He does not even take credit to his Government for their 'humane order' as to the drowning of women. Falsehood must not be imputed, if possible, to one who held so high a position; and if it be thought that even *indirectly* he denies the execution, let apology be sought for him before applying to him an odious epithet. It cannot be said that he had forgotten this case in the multitude of others he had to do with. It happened only five years before, and he was present when it was before the Privy Council. And, besides, the pamphlets which he had to answer must have brought all the circumstances of it back to his recollection. Why, then, does he ignore it altogether, neither flatly contradicting it, nor frankly admitting it ? It may be that he thought that his Government was not much to be blamed in that matter, which, *at the last*, may have been the unauthorized act of some of its too zealous officials,[1] and so not really its own act,—not an *execution* in the proper sense of the term. Or even if the execution took place under authority of the Government, Sir George may have reasoned, that in this case the sentence was carried out, only because the Government could not help it; that the Government had done all that they could to save the lives of these convicts, who at last perished from their own obstinacy in refusing to take the oath which they had petitioned for leave to take. Thus may Sir George have reasoned, when he omitted the Wigtown women from his list of female sufferers. But if it be thought that Sir George's statement cannot be thus accounted for, then let his evidence stand on the negative side of the question for what it is worth.

Sir George Mackenzie's statement needs corroboration; and accordingly Mr. Napier tells us that it is 'corroborated by *all* the diaries and reports of his Whig opponent, Fountainhall.' Such is the heading of a section of the *Case for the Crown.* How must the readers of the *Case* be surprised, when, under this heading, promising an overwhelming proof, they actually find that there is nothing about the matter in question in *any* of the said diaries and reports, and that Mr. Napier's argument in substance is: These women could not have been drowned at Wigtown, because Sir John Lauder of Fountainhall has not recorded that fact in any of his note-books ! There are surely many things true in the history of that period, and this may be one

---

[1] A pamphlet, which we shall subsequently quote, seems to allude to something of this kind.

of them, though not found in Fountainhall's voluminous *notanda*. Mr. Napier might have seen that Fountainhall's *silence* was at least as good an argument on the other side of the question. This eminent Whig lawyer was living in Edinburgh, keeping his eye on the doings of the Government, and taking notes (very fair and candid ones) of their proceedings. He was as ready to record their good deeds as their evil ones, and would doubtless have found it less laborious, and more pleasant. Their doings in the remote parts of the country, he could not always know; but what they did in Edinburgh, he was sure to be informed of. But still he has not entered it in any of his note-books among other 'memorable occurrents,' that two women, who had been sentenced at Wigtown to be drowned (that being now, through humanity of the Government, the punishment of female traitors) were at this time brought to Edinburgh, where, having confessed their wickedness and taken the oaths, they were first reprieved by the Council, and then pardoned by the King. Thus it would seem that Fountainhall's silence corroborates both sides of the question, and so can be regarded as of no weight on either side.[1]

Nor is more weight due to the omission of any special mention of this Wigtown case in the 'calumnious papers of grievances and sufferings penned by conventicle preachers' of these times. These being written, as Mr. Napier says, 'to induce the Prince of Orange to invade the kingdom,' gave a *general* statement of their wrongs and grievances, and did not profess to give all the cases of suffering in detail. Mr. Napier endeavours to convey the impression, that cases of suffering were so rare, that such a case as the Wigtown one must, if true, have been chronicled by every one who wrote regarding the persecutions of these times. But this was merely one of many atrocities. Probably, however, the allusion in the Paper of Grievances, 'from Nidsdale, Annandale, and Galloway,' is to the Wigtown women; for the statement of this provincial collector, 'that of men and *women*, merely for their opinion, who could not distinguish betwixt authority and misapplied power,' many had 'their lives taken'—is more probably an allusion to an execution of women within the district to which the paper refers, than to that of the two women in Edinburgh, as Mr. Napier contends.

It would have been more to his purpose had Mr. Napier been able to find *even one contemporary writer who has recorded a direct denial of the Wigtown execution.* This singular execution was affirmed as a fact in pamphlets published a very few years after it is said to have taken place; but Mr. Napier has not been able to find one of the numerous pamphleteers on the other side who has given it a direct contradiction. And when Wodrow's *History* was published, in

---

[1] 'The principal Parisian journal, the *Moniteur*, in the number published on the *very day* (in the year 1814) on which the allied armies are said to have entered Paris as conquerors, makes *no mention* of any such event, nor alludes at all to any military transactions, but is entirely occupied with criticisms on some *theatrical performances.*'— Whately's *Historic Doubts*, p. 79.

1722, many were still living who had perfect knowledge of the fate of the two women, and some still survived, who, having had a hand in the trial and sentence, were called on, in self-defence, to contradict Wodrow's statement, had it been 'a falsehood and a calumny.' But no one raised his voice in indignant denial. Nay, though Wodrow gave publicity to the fact that a reprieve was granted, no man in that generation attempted to prove that the reprieve was followed by a pardon. Mr. Napier himself has the honour of being the first to undertake that difficult task. It is true that, before Wodrow wrote his *History*, there were, as he himself states, those who denied or extenuated this and other cruelties of the Restoration period. Sir George Mackenzie denied it, and so did others in the same *general* way; but no one of the generation living, when the execution by drowning is said to have taken place, met that charge by a direct and explicit denial. Mr. Napier, with all his research, has not been able to find one witness on his side, except Sir George Mackenzie; and even he, as has been shown above, though answering pamphlets which charged his Government with drowning women, tied to stakes within the sea-mark, *does not venture to affirm that no such thing ever took place.*

As to the *denials* and *extenuations* of 'this matter of fact,' in which Wodrow represents some of the Jacobites of his time as having 'the impudence' to indulge, it is a remarkable circumstance, that we know of their existence only from the writings of Presbyterians *who mention them simply to confute them.* It might have been expected that Mr Napier, knowing that such denials and extenuations were current in certain circles in Wodrow's time, would have examined the Jacobite pamphlets from 1685 down to 1722, with the view of finding allusions to these denials, and of learning the grounds on which they were made. In this investigation, however, Mr. Napier, as we shall see, seems never to have engaged. The friend whose name is mentioned in the preface as having given us valuable assistance in collecting additional materials for this edition, assures us that, in a tolerably extensive and careful examination of the pamphlets of that period by writers of both parties, the only notice which he has found in any of them previous to the time of Wodrow of a denial, is, not in the writings of any Episcopalian or Jacobite pamphleteer, but in that of a Presbyterian, who, like Wodrow, mentions it only to show its groundlessness. This notice occurs in *Popery Reviving*, a pamphlet published in 1714, from which we have already given an extract describing the manner of the drowning. The author begins his account of the Wigtown case by saying, 'I shall briefly condescend only upon one instance (of the cruelty of the times), because it is ordinarily denied by a great many of our modern Jacobites, and said to be a calumny raised to asperse the late Government.' Wodrow, in 1722, used language of the same kind in his *History*, as did Patrick Walker in 1727. Mr. Napier seems to attach importance to the fact, that in Wodrow's time 'the Jacobites had the impudence, some of them, to deny, and others to extenuate, this matter of fact.' He will now learn that, at an even earlier date, such denials were in circulation. But we cannot see that his cause is thereby in any way helped. For what weight can be attached to denials, of the very existence of which we know only from the writings of those who dragged them from their obscurity merely to declare their falsehood ? One is curious to know what shape or form these denials took; for though the Jacobite party used the press very freely after the Revolution, and stoutly denied that they had ever persecuted, no one can point to a page in any of their numerous writings in which is to be found a denial of this specific case. We can point to an admission of it by one of the party, with an attempt to *extenuate its circumstances*, and to excuse the Government, but not to a denial. How, then, was it denied, since we find no trace of a denial in any publication of the time ? Not, certainly, on the house-tops, as the fact was proclaimed by those who challenged the deniers to come out of their obscurity and make good their denials before the world; it must have been whispered merely in non-juring meeting-houses and Jacobite coteries. Denial in those days, when so many actors in the tragedy were still living, durst not face the world in print. It is only in our day that it has assumed that bold and defiant shape.[1]

Mr. Napier lays great stress upon the fact, that the Commission, of which Colonel Douglas was the head, was superseded by the appointment of another Commission on the 21st April. It is not easy to see how that fact tends to prove his case in any way. Granting that Colonel Douglas's Commission for 'trying or punishing' was void at that date, it is surely not contended that those condemned on the 13th April must needs be set free on the 21st, because the power to punish had ceased to exist. In this case the Commission, after they had tried and condemned, did not exercise their power of punishing, as they were instructed to do, by having sentence executed 'immediately at the place;' but allowed their convicts to carry their case by petition to the Privy Council, who, while they granted a reprieve, still reserved the power (as the idea of a reprieve implies) of executing the sentence, should they see fit.

[1] Dr. M'Crie, in his *Review of the Tales of My Landlord*, gives the following account of the denials and extenuations which were industriously circulated by the Jacobite party after the Revolution : ' When they were restrained from torturing and murdering the Presbyterians, the Scottish Episcopalians and Jacobites, abusing the lenity of a new and tolerant Government, which they eagerly sought to overturn, took up the pen, and, with hands yet besmeared with the blood of their countrymen, employed it in writing against them calumnious invectives and scurrilous lampoons, which they industriously circulated in England, where the facts were not known, with the view of instigating the English Church to take part with them, first in preventing, and afterwards in overturning, the establishment of Presbytery in Scotland. The authors of these pamphlets were so impudent and brazen-faced as to deny that Presbyterians had been subjected to persecution for their religious opinions ; and at the same time that they were pleading for a toleration for themselves, to justify all the intolerant and barbarous measures of the two preceding reigns.'

There is no other point in Mr. Napier's argument that claims remark. No one can fail to see that his proof is inconclusive, even if there were no evidence on the other side. But it so happens that the proof on the affirmative side of the question is full and conclusive; such a proof as, according to the usually received laws of evidence, is amply sufficient to establish any historical fact.

CHAPTER III.

———

HAVING examined the proof on the *negative* side of the question, we shall now proceed to state the evidence on the affirmative side. This may be arranged under the following heads: 1*st*, Tradition; 2*d*, Early Pamphlets; 3*d*, Earlier Histories; 4*th*, Minutes of Local Church Courts; 5*th*, Monumental Evidence.

1. *Tradition.*

It is not necessary to do more than refer to the *tradition* which has handed down to successive generations in Galloway, the story of the drowning of the two women at Wigtown in 1685—a tradition which still points to the spot on the sands below the town of Wigtown where the tragedy was enacted. Tradition is not the best vehicle of *accurate* historical truth. Some circumstantial details will drop out of any narrative so transmitted, and others may be added that are at variance with the exact truth. Still, there must be a foundation in truth for the *main facts: they* cannot be completely reversed, and yet the story gain general belief in the district in which the events occurred. The *drowning* is, doubtless, the main fact in the story of Lauchlison and Wilson which tradition has handed down; and had there been no drowning in the case, there would have been no story, and the names of the two women would not have been remembered after the generation in which they lived. Their trial and sentence are facts admitted; but, had the case ended in a recantation on their part, followed by a pardon, how could it have got into general belief in Galloway, and been handed down from father to son, that they were executed in accordance with their sentence? Suppose, according to Mr. Napier's theory, that some one, in a pamphlet published a few years after, falsely and calumniously charged the Government with this execution, belief might have been produced in some living at a distance from the scene of the event; but it could never have given rise to that universal local belief in the execution which has always existed in Galloway. During the lifetime of those who, being their contemporaries, had personal knowledge of the fate of the two women, there could not have been two opinions in Galloway as to what that fate actually was. And if we suppose the non-drowning theory to have been the first and the true belief, how is the entire change from the true to the false one to be explained. A false version of history could never have taken the place of the true tradition. Shields, Defoe, and Wodrow, whatever they might have done in other parts, could never have taught the people of *Galloway* to renounce, with one accord, the account of this matter of local history which their fathers had handed down to them, and to adopt another, not merely different as to details, but contradictory as to the main fact. In place of history reversing the tradition, the reception of the history by the people of Galloway can be explained only by the fact of its being in accordance with the tradition.

And not only has there been in Galloway the universal belief in the drowning as a matter of general tradition, but in the family of the Wilsons the fact of Margaret Wilson's martyrdom has been preserved as a part of the family history. The descendants of Gilbert Wilson in Glenvernock have continued from generation to generation in the same locality, occupying the farm of Glenvernock itself, or one of those adjoining. The highly respectable and intelligent tenant of Garchew, in the parish of Penninghame, bearing both the Christian name and surname of his ancestor, Gilbert Wilson, assures us, that Margaret Wilson's cruel death was a frequent subject of conversation in his father's family, and that he never heard the received account of it called in question, till it recently became a subject of controversy. This gentleman's father, John Wilson, who was tenant of Glenvernock for forty-nine years, died in 1841, at the age of eighty-three. He was consequently born in 1758—that is, only twenty-four years after the death of Thomas Wilson, the martyr's brother, who, as will be shown, lived till 1734. There are thus between the present representative of the family and Thomas Wilson, only two intervening links in the chain of tradition, viz. his father and grandfather, the latter of whom, doubtless, had the true story from Thomas Wilson, in whose mouth it was not a matter of tradition, but of personal knowledge.

2. *Early Pamphlets.*

Mr. Napier, as has been shown, is so unreasonable as to argue that, if the execution at Wigtown be a fact, it must have been noticed by *every one* who wrote about the events of the period. It would have been an argument deserving of some consideration had he been able to say that *no* writer in the years immediately succeeding the date of the alleged martyrdom alluded to it. That, however, cannot be said; for it is mentioned just where we might have expected—that is, in the papers and pamphlets written to expose the proceedings of the Restoration Government.

It is probably referred to in the minutes of the Society People (the Cameronians) the very year it took place. These manuscript minutes, still in possession of the Reformed Presbyterian Synod, were published in 1780, under the title of *Faithful Contendings*. In the narrative connecting the minute of 12th February with that of 28th May 1685, this statement occurs: 'Yea, women, and that both old and young, escaped not their bloody and barbarous hands, by whom some were *strangely murdered*, and many of them carried to prison.'[1]

The *Informatory Vindication*, written by Renwick, submitted to the Societies in 1686, and published by them the following year, contains this undoubted reference to the Wigtown execution: 'Drowning women, some of them very young, and some of exceeding old age!'

The pamphlet, *A Hind let Loose*, written, it is said, by Alexander Shields, and published by the Societies in 1687, has, as has been shown above, a statement very clearly referring to the execution at Wigtown: 'Neither were women spared; but some were hanged, some drowned tied to stakes within the sea-mark, to be devoured gradually with the growing waves, and some of them of a very young, some of an old, age.'[2]

The following passage from the Prince of Orange's Declaration for Scotland (quoted at length by Wodrow, vol. iv. p. 470), dated at The Hague, 10th October 1688, shows that he was led to believe that *drowning* was one of the modes of execution that had not only been ordained by law, but had actually been put in practice in Scotland: 'Empowering officers and soldiers to act upon the subject living in quiet and full peace, the greatest barbarities, in destroying them by hanging, shooting, and *drowning* them, without any form of law, or respect to age or sex, not giving some of them time to pray to God for mercy; and this for no other reason but because they would not answer or satisfy them in such questions as they proposed to them, without any warrant of law, and against the common interest of mankind, which frees all men from being obliged to discover their secret thoughts.' Thus, at this early date, the Prince of Orange, in a public manifesto, named *drowning* as one of the 'barbarities' of the Government; and will any believe that he did so on the single testimony of Shields? He must have had good and ample testimony before he made such a charge.

[1] *Reformed Presbyterian Magazine* for March 1863, p. 93. A writer in the *Edinburgh Courant* (23d August 1867), reviewing our first edition (the only hostile critic of the press we have had), charges us, or rather the *Reformed Presbyterian Magazine*, which we followed, with quoting, as a proof of the martyrdom, a minute written five days *before it*. What we quoted was not a minute tied to a date, but a *narrative* connecting two minutes, and written, we should suppose, at or just before the date of the letter. We have not been able to see this pamphlet; but one whom we believe to be a good authority assures us, that the reviewer is quite wrong in this small criticism, and that on the 6th May, which he fixes as the date of the extract, there was no minute, but an agreement to adjourn to the 28th May. The testimony in the above extract is not a direct one, and it might be omitted without the slightest damage to our proof; still it is *highly probable* that the phrase 'strangely murdered,' as applied to *women, old and young*, refers to the Wigtown case; for *drowning*, as a capital punishment, was *strange* in Scotland (according to Pitcairn, it was in force in the 15th and 16th centuries.—*Trials*, vol. i. p. 152, note); and other forms of death at that time were far from being so.

[2] *A Hind let Loose* is a book of 742 pages, though we call it a pamphlet. The quotation is at p. 197 of the first edition.

In another pamphlet (already quoted), also published by the Societies in 1690, and entitled, *A Short Memorial of Sufferings and Grievances*, the Wigtown tragedy is expressly mentioned: '*Item*, The said Colonel or Lieutenant-General James Douglas, together with the laird of Lag and Captain Winram, most illegally condemned, and most inhumanly drowned at stakes within the sea-mark, two women at Wigtown, viz. Margaret Lachlan, upwards of sixty years, and Margaret Wilson, about twenty years of age, the foresaid fatal year 1685.' Here, within five years after the event, the case of the Wigtown sufferers is plainly given to the public, and three of the agents concerned in their condemnation pointed out by name. Though this pamphlet was a manifesto of the Society People, it was written by Alexander Shields, and Mr. Napier endeavours to break its force by heaping abuse on Shields' character. It is not necessary to this argument, in which we are dealing merely with the facts of the case, to show that Shields was either a wise or a good man, or that he wrote in polished terms and in a Christian spirit. The pamphlet in question was adopted by a considerable section of the people, and published by them as *their* memorial of sufferings and grievances; and, however anxious they may have been to defame the Government, it is not easy to imagine that they would have been so infatuated as to give a *specific* case of suffering, mentioning the circumstances of time, place, and persons concerned, if the story was utterly false, and one that could only damage their cause by being at once denied and disproved,—which it was not.[1]

Mr. Napier says that Shields ' did not venture to make that *specific* statement in 1687 (in his pamphlet, *A Hind, etc.*), when most probably the two women were known to be alive; but in 1690, emboldened by the advent of King William, ere which time the women may have died or *become expatriated*,' he put forth this other pamphlet, in which the Wigtown martyrdom ' makes its first appearance.'[2] Mr. Napier's theory demands that the two women, though not drowned, should be speedily put out of the way; and for that purpose he suggests one or other of two modes of exit—neither of them, it will be allowed, improbable. After the trials and sufferings to which they were subjected, who can wonder that even the younger did not survive five years ? or, at all events, at a time when so many were sent to the plantations to be sold as slaves, at once to free the Government of troublesome subjects, and to enrich the faithful servants of the Crown, who can wonder that two women, who were actually sentenced to death for their evil courses, should at least ' become expatriated ? ' So, according to Mr. Napier, Shields and the Cameronians, no longer afraid of being contradicted by the two women in person, now ' venture ' to publish that enormous lie, the Wigtown martyrdom; utterly forgetful, it would

---

[1] It is worth noticing, that the *Short Memorial* gives a list amounting to seventy-eight of those who suffered death during the 'killing time,' and that no case has ever been challenged except that of the Wigtown women.

[2] *Case for the Crown*, p. 82.

seem, that they were still liable to be contradicted by the three judges whose names they had mentioned, and by Lords of the Privy Council whose clemency they had aspersed, and by Sir George Mackenzie, at this time about to take up his 'able pen' to write his vindication of the Government; for Shields could not foresee that Sir George was to die the following year, and never set eyes on his 'rubbish.'

In 1690 there was published in London a pamphlet, entitled *A Brief and True Account of the Sufferings of the Church of Scotland occasioned by the Episcopalians since* 1660, which was a reply to an Episcopalian pamphlet called *The Present State and Condition of the Clergy and Church of Scotland.* The author of the *Brief Account*, in replying to a statement in *The Present State* to the effect ' that it's beyond the power of words to express their misery to that degree as they suffer it,' says, ' But I would have him to remember that there are Episcopal inhumanities which we have felt of a far higher nature than those he falsely alleges they suffer, viz. rapine, murder, hanging, *drowning*, beheading, famine, torturing with boot, thumikins.'

The next work in the order of dates to be noticed as containing an express mention of the execution at Wigtown, is, *A Second Vindication of the Church of Scotland*, being an answer to Five Pamphlets, the titles of which are set down after the preface. By the author of the former *Vindication*, in answer to ten questions. Printed at Edinburgh, 1691.[1] This is a book of 204 pages 4to, and contains at page 128 a notice of the Wigtown case in the following terms :—' Some gentlemen (whose names, out of respect for them, I forbear to mention) took two women—Margaret Lauchland and Margaret Wilson, the one of sixty, the other of twenty years—and caused them be tyed to a stake within the sea-mark, at Wigtown, and left them there till the tyde overflowed them, and drowned them; and this was done without any legal trial, 1685.'

It was not the design of this book to set forth the persecutions which had been endured by the Presbyterians, but to meet the charges of persecution and ill-usage now made against them by the Jacobite and Episcopalian party, especially in connection with the ejection and rabbling of the clergy. The pamphlets, to which this book was an answer, set forth in exaggerated terms the sufferings to which the Episcopalian clergy were subjected at the Revolution. In such a crisis things do not usually run very smoothly, and they whose errors have rendered a revolution necessary are likely to be sufferers. Many of the clergy had made themselves so odious to the people, that when there was an *interregnum*, and no law in the land, the mob took the law into their own hands, and ejected not a few of the ministers, sometimes with violence, and generally without ceremony. It was the design of the Five Pamphlets to make the most of these cases; and it was the design of the *Second Vindication* to meet these charges. But the author of one of the pamphlets, *A Letter concerning the Sufferings*

---

[1] The *First Vindication* was published also in 1691, and *A Defence of the Vindication* in 1694.

E

of the Episcopal Clergy in Scotland, had attempted ' a vindication of the Episcopal clergy from provoking the Presbyterians, or having any hand in their persecutions in the late reigns.' He had said : ' The clergy can defy them to give one instance where any Dissenters suffered death, or was in any way injured by the information or instigation of any minister in Scotland.' He had affirmed that ' they were neither judges, nor parties, nor witnesses, nor accusers,'—that ' when they were commanded, by authority, to give in the names of Dissenters, they generally declined it, till they were forced to it,'—that ' no Dissenters suffered purely for dissenting, but only in case of open rebellion, or in case of murder.' These strong assertions (evidently designed for readers south of the Tweed) the author of the *Second Vindication* answers, and, out of many, he gives three cases as a specimen, doubtless selecting those that were well known,—the Wigtown case, that of Thomas Richard of Cumnock, and that of John Brown of Priesthill. If he had had the curates' lists of Penninghame and Kirkinner, and the synodical acts of the Bishop of Galloway to refer to, his answer would have been more complete.

It is of importance to know who was the author of the *Second Vindication.* Mr. Napier informs us, on the authority of *The Scots Presbyterian Eloquence,* that he was ' Mr. Rule, who calls himself a doctor of medicine, for they never pretend to have any in divinity.' ' Rule,' Mr. Napier informs us on his own authority, ' was a Presbyterian hack, but rather shy, and inclined to bolt,' [1]—a pamphleteer of the ' same stamp' as Shields, whose words he merely ' copied.' [2] Thus does Mr. Napier introduce to the notice of his readers Dr. Gilbert Rule, at that time Principal of the University of Edinburgh, and minister of the Old Greyfriars, formerly sub-Principal of Aberdeen. Surely Mr. Napier does not pay sufficient respect to the Head of a university. It may be well, therefore, to state that Dr. Rule's eminence was acknowledged by the men of his time of both sides, and that the ablest and most learned of the Episcopal party did not think it beneath them to enter the lists in controversy with him. Even John Sage (afterwards a bishop), one of the most learned Scotchmen of his day, wrote a book of 562 pages in reply to one by Rule, entitled *The Cyprianick Bishop Examined, and found not to be a Diocesan.* Nor do the Principal's *shying* and *bolting* propensities (if such he had) seem to have rendered him unsafe and unserviceable in the Presbyterian ranks ; for we find that he was appointed by the General Assembly of 1690 (Sessio 25) to reply to the aforesaid pamphlets, and that the *Second Vindication* was actually written at the bidding of the Church of Scotland. As the Church and Government of Scotland were unjustly aspersed by these pamphlets, published in London and circulated in England, it was deemed proper to answer them. Rule was appointed to do this service ; and ministers throughout the country were ordered to give him the necessary information regarding the cases of cruelty (*rabbling,* as they were termed) which were alleged.

[1] *Case for the Crown,* p. 86.   [2] *Ibid.,* p. 82.

It is to these, and not to the few cases of persecution of Presbyterians, which are mentioned only incidentally, that he alludes in his preface (which Mr. Napier quotes) when he says, ' that the truth of matters of fact asserted in this treatise are not to be taken from me, but from those who are my informers'—from those ministers who were instructed to send him information as to what had really taken place in those cases of ejection and rabbling of which he was appointed to treat.

How or where Dr. Rule got his knowledge of the Wigtown case really matters very little—not even though he had copied it from Shields. For the value of his notice of the case does not depend upon his personal knowledge; at least it has a value independent of that. The strength of the proof arising from his assertion of the martyrdom evidently lies in these circumstances—that, being a man of mark, and one especially appointed to vindicate his Church, his work had a wide circulation, and attracted the attention of those on the other side, and actually called forth distinct replies *from three of their ablest writers, none of whom denied his assertion in the Wigtown case.* These were, Robert Calder, Dr. Monro, and the famous John Sage himself.

Calder's work, the notorious *Scotch Presbyterian Eloquence,* was published in 1693. Its title page promises remarks on the late vindication of the kirk, and these occur pp. 53–67. He quotes the very pages before and after those containing the account of the Presbyterian persecutions, but these he leaves without remark. He leaves Rule's ' eloquence' on these tender points without criticism.

Almost immediately afterwards George Ridpath published in London *An Answer to Scotch Presbyterian Eloquence,* in which the Wigtown case was repeated in similar terms to those used by Dr. Rule.

. In the same year, 1693, Dr. Monro, ex-Principal of Edinburgh, who, Mr. Napier tells us, was ' Dundee's accomplished friend and eulogist,' published *An Apology for the Clergy of Scotland,* a pamphlet of 108 pages, devoting 84 pages to Rule's *Vindication,* and 24 pages of postscript to Ridpath's *Answer.* Monro goes over the *Vindication* page by page, disputing the accuracy of many of Rule's *statements,* and controverting his arguments ; but he lets the Presbyterian sufferings pass unnoticed, and denies neither the drowning of the Wigtown women, nor the shooting of John Brown, though the latter case especially, told by Rule with all its aggravating circumstances, must have provoked Dundee's ' friend and eulogist ' (as it has another eulogist of Dundee in recent times) to attempt, if not a denial, at least an explanation in mitigation. But he attempts nothing of the kind. Neither does he, when dealing with Ridpath, notice the Wigtown case, though he defends the conventicle laws as necessary, and asserts that no one in that period suffered death except for high treason ; thus virtually admitting that those said by Ridpath to have been put to death, had actually suffered, but, in his opinion, suffered deservedly, as guilty of treason. The ex-Principal, too, praises and defends Sir George Mackenzie's *Vindication,* of which he himself was the editor ;

but he fails to find in it *proof* that the Wigtown women were not executed, else he probably would have anticipated Mr. Napier in the publication of that discovery.

Third in order, and though last, not least, John Sage, in 1695, published his *Fundamental Charter of Presbytery, etc.*, the preface of which (96 pages) is devoted to ' G. R., the Vindicator of the kirk, who is freely put in mind of his habitual infirmities.' More minutely even than Calder or Monro does Sage go over the *Second Vindication.* He fills several pages with Rule's strong expressions, to put him in mind of his ' infirmities,' making quotations alarmingly near the recorded martyrdom; and we feel relieved when he passes over the page of Presbyterian sufferings without saying, ' Here we have " a calumnious tissue of monstrous fables," ' or something of like import. He allows the Vindicator's three specimen cases to pass without comment, either on their style or matter. At first sight, it may surprise us that Sage and the other two critics should have allowed Rule's version of the Wigtown case to pass so easily; for he had evidently fallen into two popular errors which they could perhaps have corrected. He was wrong, first as to the *mode* of drowning, and he was wrong again in saying that the women were executed ' without any legal trial.' If they knew better, why did they not correct him? Probably because they could not correct these circumstantial errors without directly admitting the main fact, which they were too prudent to do. It was not their policy to spread the knowledge of such cases, even though they had been able to give a mitigated version of them. They dealt largely in *general* denials, but did not venture to condescend to particular instances.[1]

We come next to notice certain pamphlets, of 1703, which were for the first time, in this controversy, quoted in the *Scotsman* newspaper, after the publication of our first edition. Our researches had been exclusively directed to the local sources of proof, chiefly to the records of the church courts. We had no opportunity of searching old pamphlets for new testimonies, and would not have presumed to follow Mr. Napier in that line of investigation, in the hope of making further discoveries, seeing that he had proclaimed that he had ' paused long enough and searched deep enough, to justify some confidence that no deeper researches are likely to restore the credit of this calumnious

---

[1] We have dwelt longer on Dr. Rule's testimony than the exigencies of our argument require, but we were anxious to state it at length, as well illustrating an important canon of historical evidence, viz., *When a thing is asserted as a fact, and brought fully under the notice of those who have a strong interest in disproving it, and who, though they controvert other things, leave this one without dispute, there is the highest degree of moral certainty that that thing is true.* Of course the difficulty is to *apply* the laws of evidence,— to see that we have really, in any given case, all the required conditions of the law. This difficulty will render even the best canons that can be framed an imperfect guide to truth. Were it otherwise, as Archbishop Whately remarks, man would have conferred on him ' the unattainable attribute of infallibility.' But though we cannot have an infallible guide, we should accept the best we can have; and the chapter of Logic which treats of the ' Laws of Evidence,' deserves more study than it receives in our times.

romance.'[1] We concluded, therefore, that he had thoroughly examined all the controversial writings of the period, so that any admission of the disputed fact by an Episcopalian author we never dreamed
of. · We felt, too, that one or two additional notices in Presbyterian
pamphlets would not have added much to the weight of the proof, for
those already quoted in the controversy were sufficient to show that
the fact in question had been affirmed on the one side, and, so far as
known, not attempted to be disproved on the other, from its date
downwards till 1711, when it was certified in the records of the church
courts by those who had personal knowledge of it; and so established
by a proof which no reasonable man capable of estimating evidence
could say was insufficient.

Knowing, however, how slow some are to believe what is clear
enough to others, it was with no little satisfaction, as well as surprise,
that, shortly after the publication of our pamphlet, we received a
letter from a clergyman of the Church of Scotland, stating that he had
in his possession a pamphlet, by *an Episcopalian writer, admitting the
drowning of the two women at Wigtown.* This tract is entitled ' A Short
Character of the Presbyterian Spirit, in so far as it can be gathered out
of their own Books, especially out of a Letter from a Gentleman to a
Member of Parliament, etc.' It was printed in 1703, but the name of
neither printer nor author is given. We recommended that an extract relating to the Wigtown case should be sent to the newspapers,
as the subject was at the time exciting attention. This was accordingly done, and immediately afterwards there appeared an article in
the *Scotsman* (the second of the two already referred to) showing that
this pamphlet was printed by Mr. Andrew Symson,[2] who at the time
of the martyrdom was Episcopalian minister of Kirkinner (Margaret
Lauchlison's parish), and was afterwards a printer in Edinburgh; and
that the reputed author was his son, Mr. Matthias Symson,[3] then a

---

[1] *Case for the Crown* (Preface, p. viii).

[2] In the first edition we stated that Mr. Symson left Kirkinner in the end of 1684,
but in this we were mistaken. From certain memoranda in the preface of his *Tripatriarchicon*, it appears that he went to Kirkinner in 1663, and lived there ' about the
space of twenty-three years,' that is, till 1686. He then went to Douglas, where he was
instituted as minister 12th January 1686, and where he continued till he was rabbled
out by the populace some time previous to 20th October ·1691. For some years subsequently he seems to have devoted himself to literary pursuits. Towards the end of the
century he came to Edinburgh, where, as appears from Watson's *History of the Art of
Printing*, Edinburgh, 1713, p. 18, he was a printer from 1700 till his death in 1712,
having taken up the business when his son Matthias had commenced.

[3] Mr. Matthias Symson, after he completed his studies, went to England. He was
rector of Moorby, Lincolnshire, and afterwards of Wennington, Essex. He was also a
canon of Lincoln. He obtained the degree of D.D. from Edinburgh University in 1738,
and died in 1742. In 1738 he edited a new edition of *The Present State of Scotland*,—
an interesting work, and containing many valuable notices of ecclesiastical matters from
the Restoration to the Revolution. Several letters addressed by him to Dr. Zachary
Grey, about the years 1734–38, may be found in Nichol's *Literary History*, iv. 357. They
are interesting as showing that his early dislike of Presbytery, as displayed in the *Short
Character*, remained strong to the last.

student of divinity, and living with his father. Mr. Symson was minister of Kirkinner from 1663 to 1686, and in October 1684 had affixed to Margaret Lauchlison's name the epithet *disorderly* (to intimate that she was a transgressor of the church laws) in the list of parishioners above twelve years of age, which he was by law obliged to give to the authorities. He was still resident at Kirkinner (three miles from Wigtown) in May following, when the execution is said to have taken place. His son Matthias is not included in his father's list in 1684, which shows that he was then under twelve years of age; but as he took his degree in the University of Edinburgh 23d June 1699, he must have been old enough in 1685 to remember anything remarkable in connection with his father's parish which then took place. It will therefore be allowed, that a pamphlet written by Mr. Symson, junior, when living in his father's house in 1703, and proceeding from his father's printing press, is the best testimony that could have turned up on the subject of the martyrdom; and if the writing and printing of this tract can be brought home to the Symsons, an *admission* of the disputed fact by *them* is the best possible reproof to Mr. Napier for having accused the Presbyterian minister and elders of Kirkinner of having 'sealed with prayer an abominable falsehood,' when, seven years afterwards, they recorded in their session minutes the sufferings of Margaret Lauchlison.

The writer in the *Scotsman* informs us, that when he saw the extract from the *Short Character* quoted in the newspapers, he made search for the pamphlet, and was so fortunate as to obtain from David Laing, Esq., a volume containing it, and thirty-seven other tracts, most of them printed in 1703. This volume has, at the beginning, a manuscript index in the handwriting of the day, and most of the anonymous tracts are ascribed to those who were their reputed authors. The name of the author, in several cases, is written on the pamphlet itself, as well as given in the index. This is the case as regards the *Short Character*, which, both in the index and on the pamphlet itself, is said to be by Mr. Matthias Symson.

There is, besides, in the pamphlet itself the strongest internal evidence that it was written, not only by a keen party man on the Episcopal side, but by one who, like Symson, had the most complete knowledge of the Wigtown case—who could correct the errors of the popular belief regarding it, and who even promises that he might still make a further revelation, for the clearing of ' the then Governours' from the blame unjustly laid upon them. There are, too, references to *Galloway* matters, and to what took place at *Douglas* (to which place the Symsons went when they left Kirkinner), which all tend to confirm the testimony of the manuscript index.

The proof as to the printer is even stronger than that as to the author. Watson's *History of the Art of Printing* shows who were at that time printers in Edinburgh; and of the five then carrying on that business, it was almost a matter of course that Mr. Andrew Symson, himself an ejected Episcopalian minister, should have been employed in printing any tracts on the Episcopal side of the controversy which was then being carried on ; and certainly he was the person to print any pamphlet written by his son. In Mr. Laing's volume there is just *one* pamphlet which bears on its title page the name of Andrew Symson as printer. This pamphlet, and the *Short Character*, and others in the volume by Episcopal authors, as well as a volume written and printed by Andrew Symson (*The Tripatriarchicon*), were submitted by the writer in the *Scotsman* (as he tells us) to two practical printers, and 'they both unhesitatingly said that, judging from the peculiar scroll ornamentation or head-lines which they contain, and from certain specialities connected with the types, they must all have been printed from the same fount, and that the types of the other pamphlets in the volume were all different.'

We have been favoured, through Mr. Laing's kindness, with an opportunity of examining this volume, and can confirm the statements of the writer in the *Scotsman*. On the evidence of this volume, there can be no doubt who was the printer of the *Short Character*. The question who was its author may not be so clearly solved, as we cannot tell who wrote the index, and what opportunities he had of knowing who wrote the several tracts which form the volume ; but we may be sure (even if we had no further proof), that whoever wrote the tract in question, had the benefit of Mr. Andrew Symson's knowledge of the Wigtown case, and that an *admission of the execution* of one of his former parishioners and near neighbours would not have issued from Mr. Symson's press, if he had known that no such execution ever took place.[1]

But there is still stronger proof than that afforded by Mr. Laing's volume, that Mr. Symson was the printer, and his son the writer, of the *Short Character*. There are in the Advocates' Library, Edinburgh, several volumes of pamphlets (which were pointed out to us by Mr. Gordon, who had previously examined them), bearing the book-plate and autograph signature of the Honourable Archibald Campbell. Volumes I., II., and III. contain 104 pamphlets, almost all published in 1703–4, and apparently a complete collection of the pamphlets of these two controversial years. Mr. Campbell must have been an accurate and methodical man, for he marks at the beginning of each volume what he paid for each pamphlet ; and at the end of volume III. there is the following entry—' These papers were bound together, Nov. 15, 1704, at Edinburgh,'—adding to the total for the pamphlets the sum which the binding of each of the three volumes cost. He gives at the end of each volume indexes in his own handwriting, and mentions, in most cases, the name of the author of each of the tracts,—in the case of Presbyterian authors, generally adding epithets far from complimentary. The *Short Character* is ascribed to Mr. Matthias

---

[1] The above is a mere abstract of the proof as to the author and printer of the *Short Character*, given in the *Scotsman's* elaborate article (4th September 1867), which is a remarkable example of that careful investigation, which the author of the *Case for the Crown* complains has been hitherto neglected by writers of Scottish history.

Symson, both in the index, and on the tract itself. In every instance the names of authors given by Mr. Campbell, agree with those given in Mr. Laing's volume.[1]

In Mr. Campbell's volumes there is a considerable number of pamphlets bearing the name of Andrew Symson as printer, and these are invariably characterized by the same ornamental scroll and other peculiarities of typography as the *Short Character*, showing even to an unpractised eye that *it*, as well as the others, proceeded from Mr. Symson's press.

Mr. Campbell's testimony as to the authorship of this tract is invaluable; for it is well known who he was, and what opportunities he must have had of information. He was the grandson of the Marquis of Argyle, who was beheaded in 1661, and the son of Lord Neil Campbell and Lady Vere Kerr. He was a staunch Episcopalian, and was afterwards one of the non-juring bishops in Scotland, and is notorious as the person who carried off the original records of the Church of Scotland, commonly called *The Booke of the Universall Kirke*, and gifted them to Zion College, London, on condition that it would neither part with them, nor allow any transcript to be taken. In 1703 he was resident in Edinburgh—a prominent man in the controversies of the day—a writer of pamphlets himself, and well able to tell who were the writers on both sides, especially on his own side. That he knew, and had dealings with Andrew Symson, who was the printer of all the Episcopal tracts published in Edinburgh at that time, cannot be doubted; and no man was more likely to know all the secrets of the authorship of the pamphlets of the day. Mr. Campbell's indexes, therefore, giving the names of the authors of anonymous tracts, may be regarded as an excellent authority on any question as to the authorship of any pamphlet of that day, especially of those on the Episcopal side; and when we have his handwriting to assure us that Matthias Symson wrote the *Short Character* (especially when we have another concurring testimony), we may consider that point to be as well proved as any question of anonymous authorship can be.

Having settled the question of authorship, we may now quote Mr. Matthias Symson's testimony, looking first to the circumstances which called it forth. The subject of dispute in 1703 was *Toleration*,—a subject on which neither side seems to have had very enlightened views. The Episcopal party had not illustrated that subject by their practice in the former reigns, and they felt it all the more difficult to teach the lesson which they had failed to exemplify. After the Revolution, neither side did much to promote that Christian temper out of which toleration will naturally spring. Both sides employed the press freely, and a rapid fire of angry pamphlets was interchanged. On the one side came out *Toleration Defended*, and this was answered in *Toleration's Fence Removed*. The author of this tract (Mr. James

---

[1] In cataloguing the library, these three volumes have unfortunately been separated. They may be found as follows: Vol. I. under Pamphlets, $\frac{1}{131}$; vol. II., $\frac{1}{313}$; vol. III., $\frac{1}{500}$.

Ramsay of Eyemouth, afterwards of Kelso, and Moderator of the General Assembly in 1738 and 1741), after giving an account of the laws against nonconformity in the previous reigns, has the following passage, pp. 7, 8 :—

' It is well enough known that poor women were executed in the *Grassmercat :* sure it was not for rising in arms against the King : others of them were tyed to stakes within flood-mark till the sea came up and drowned them, and this without any form or process of Law. How many were by souldiers taken up by the way, or while they were about their Employments, examined on this or the other head, and if the common souldiers were not satisfied with their answers, they shot them dead on the spot: how many Worthy Gentlemen were fined even above the value of their fortunes, merely because a Presbyterian Minister preached or prayed in their families : yea, though the Gentlemen observed the law themselves, if their ladies, though never so privately, went to hear a Presbyterian Minister, their husbands were harassed and broken.'

Mr. Symson's *Short Character* was in reply to this tract and some others on the same side ; and the reference to the Wigtown case, in the passage above quoted, is thus commented on, pp. 6, 7 :—

' He says: " *Others were tyed to stakes within the flood-mark till the sea came up and drowned them, and this without any form or Process of Law.*" He durst not instance any so treated. I know they generally talk of two women in *Galloway,*— drowned they were indeed, but not *tyed to stakes within the flood-mark till the sea came up,* as this malicious Vindicator misrepresents, who, it seems, has had no better informer than the frontispiece of that Lying, pestiferous, and rebellious Lybel, *A Hind let Loose;* and what he adds, *without any form or process of law,* is so manifest a Lye, that hundreds in *Galloway* can testify the contrary. They were judicially condemned after the usual Solemnities of Procedure. The Judges were several gentlemen commissioned by authority, of whom Mr. D. G., brother to the then L. of Cl. [that is, evidently, Mr. David Graham, brother to the then Laird of Claverhouse], was one. The Chancellor of Assise (or Foreman of the jury) and Clerk of the Court are yet alive. And though the Records of that Court should be lost, yet the Registers of the Privy Council can clear the matter on this point, so that this may for ever stop the lying mouths of such vain bablers, busiebodies, and impudent Calumniators who say that they were drowned without form or Process of Law. And, furthermore, if the vindicator, or any man, shall duly and impartially consider all the circumstances of that affair (a particular account whereof may be hereafter made publick), they will not be very hasty to exclaim against the then Governours. Neither can he or any mortal prove that the Episcopal Clergy had a hand in that matter, by accusation, information, or any manner of way.'

The author of *Toleration's Fence Removed* immediately published *An Examination of three Prelatical Pamphlets, etc.,* one of these being the *Short Character ;* and Mr. Symson's account of the Wigtown execution is thus replied to, p. 38 :—

' At pages 6 and 7 he takes upon him to deny that the poor women spoken of, T. F. R., p. 8 [*Toleration's Fence Removed*], were tyed to stakes within the floodmark till the sea came up and drowned them ; and yet I have a paper from eye-and-ear witnesses of that abominable fact; yea, and though the souldiers, by virtue of an order from the Council, made some sham triall before they did thus execute these women, it may be well said they died without any due form or process of law ; and nothing can be more unaccountable than to grant such a power to souldiers to kill whomsoever they met on the road or found at their work, if they would not give them satisfaction in such matters as they were allowed to interrogate them upon ; and not a few were thus summarily executed.'

Little need be said in the way of comment on these extracts. The fact of the execution is asserted on the one side, and admitted on the other, by one who had the very best means of knowing the truth, and who could not deny it. And it is not difficult to see how Mr. Matthias Symson was led to make an admission, which no others of his party seem to have done in their published writings. The case was one in which he had a personal interest, and of which he had personal knowledge; and he felt aggrieved by the wrong version of it which had got into circulation. We may suppose that it was not without hesitation that he penned the words, '*Drown'd they were indeed.*' But as his pamphlet was to circulate among those who knew that to be the fact, he thought it best, we presume, to admit what was notorious, so that he might be enabled to correct what he knew to be contrary to fact in the story that was very generally believed. The *manner* of the execution generally believed, he denies; and, as we have shown in the previous chapter, there is a probable reason for his doing so, though it may seem a small matter to dispute about. That the execution took place without any form or process of law, he also denies; and in this, too, he was right, for there was a law, and there were judges and a jury, and the other requisites of a legal trial.

At the same time, his opponent was not without grounds for his assertion that the execution was illegal, and after a sham trial by the soldiers, for the reprieve had suspended the legal sentence; and if the soldiers had received no order from the Council to execute the sentence, but took it upon themselves to do so, *after consultation*, that may have appeared to be a trial, and may have given currency to the story very generally believed. We do not think there was any new trial, sham or otherwise; but we may suppose that, on the reception of the reprieve, Major Winram, and those who acted with him, had the women brought up to the court-room to test them with the oath; and, on their refusing, there must of necessity have been a *consultation*, and a *decision* come to, whether or not they should execute the sentence already passed; and this, in the eyes of some onlookers, may have seemed a sham trial, and been so represented. It will be seen, however, that the intelligent men who, in 1711, composed the kirk-sessions of the parishes to which the women belonged, did not fall into that error.

Thus it appears that in 1703 the execution was a fact admitted on the Episcopalian side,—admitted, too, by those on that side who were of all others the best informed regarding it. All the dispute was regarding the *mode* of the execution, and whether it was according to a *legal sentence*. On these points Mr. Matthias Symson was in the right; but in charity we must suppose him, when he penned the last sentence of the above extract, to have been in ignorance of the lists of parishioners of Kirkinner and Penninghame handed to the authorities at Wigtown in October 1684.

The only other pamphlet (new in this controversy) which has turned up, is *Popery Reviving, etc.*, printed in Edinburgh, 1714,—valu-

able chiefly from its casting light on the *mode* of the execution.   But
as an extract has been given from it in the previous chapter to illustrate that point, it need not again be quoted.

3. *Earlier Histories.*

The first attempt to collect the sufferings of the people of Scotland
under the Restoration Government into a historical form, was made
by the Society People, and resulted in the publication of the *Cloud of
Witnesses* in 1714.[1]   In this work the history of the Wigtown execution is fully given.   There is a mistake in the date of the execution
—probably a misprint—the year '84 being put for '85 ; and it may be
that the narrative is inaccurate in some of its details.   But it is utterly
inconceivable that the main fact of the case—the drowning—is simply
an invention.   No body of men, however wickedly bent on calumniating their adversaries, could have published such a falsehood, while
those were still living who knew the truth.

Three years later, in 1717, the *Memoirs of the Church of Scotland,*
by Defoe, was published, giving a detailed account of the execution in
question.   Defoe came to Scotland in 1706, and his book, though not
published till 1717, was compiled in 1708.   Like the ancient historians, he personally collected the materials of his work on the spot,
from the best sources of information.   He states in his preface that he
had ' applied himself by books, by just authorities, by oral tradition,
by living witnesses, and by all other rational means, to make himself
sufficiently master of the matters of fact, and to endeavour to restore
the general knowledge of these great transactions to the use of poste-
rity, till some more large and particular account of them shall appear.
I shall say nothing of the performance but this, that I have endeavoured carefully to adhere to truth of fact, and to have it told as
evidently and clearly that it may not be misunderstood by the ignorant,
nor misrepresented by the malicious part of mankind in ages to come.'
Defoe's testimony on the matter in question is all the more valuable,
because it is that of an impartial inquirer.   He wrote his book, not to
serve the ends of a party, but to serve the cause of truth ; and though
he could have no personal knowledge of what was done at Wigtown
twenty-one years before, it is altogether inconceivable, if he took the
smallest trouble to ascertain what was really the fate of the two
women (as he says he did[2]), that he could have been so far imposed
upon as to be made to believe that they were drowned by the officials
of the late Government, if the fact was that they were actually pardoned and set free.

[1] The minutes of the Societies show that this work was resolved on in 1699, and
instructions given from time to time for carrying out the resolution.—*Reformed Presbyterian Magazine,* March 1863, p. 94.

[2] He says, p. 227, ' As I have received this story from creditable witnesses, take it
as follows.'

4. *Minutes of the local Church Courts.*[1]

The truth of the Wigtown martyrdom does not rest merely on the authority of anonymous pamphlets, and of memorials of those times gathered from hearsay, and authenticated by the name of no one who had the means of personal knowledge. There is the testimony of those who had the best means of knowing the fact in question—of those who were the contemporaries and fellow-parishioners of the sufferers—in the still preserved minutes of the Kirk-Sessions of Kirkinner and Penninghame, the parishes to which the women respectively belonged. This is manifestly the chief branch of the evidence; and as it has never yet been laid before the public so fully as its importance claims, the reader, it is hoped, will give what follows his patient perusal.

Mr. Napier is at great pains to show, after his own fashion, 'how the falsehood of the drowning of the women at Wigtown, first published in 1690, came to be revived in the eighteenth century, by the collectors of sufferings for Wodrow's *History.*' He would have his readers believe that these men of the eighteenth century could have no personal knowledge of those things which they have recorded as matters of fact; but that, inspired by fanatical zeal, and little under the restraint of truth and honesty, they gathered up what were then merely matters of tradition lingering in the dim and indistinct recollection of the aged, and out of legends in which there was more of falsehood than truth, fabricated the materials of a history designed to calumniate the fallen dynasty. But to guard against any misrepresentation of his views, let Mr. Napier tell, in his own terms, how the records of sufferings were got up by the courts of the Church of Scotland. 'The parochial process of collecting was ingenious and certain of success. Starting with the postulate that the Governments of the Restoration had followed one undeviating course and progress of injustice, oppression, and cruelty, opposed to patriotic integrity, Christian sanctity, and rural innocence, every statement or story was at once received and adopted for truth, whatever the source, if only it were sufficiently defamatory to illustrate with effect the great mother-calumny. Accordingly the ladle was sent round all the " suffering" parishes, by order of the tribunals of the kirk, collecting this species of contribution chiefly from aged men and women, who were invalids and paupers. But all were expected to contribute a suffering, however small, to this grand *commination* against the fallen dynasty. The head-collector was the minister of the parish. What old mumper could withstand the minister? Out of blindness, deafness, doitedness, crabbedness, and coughing, he extracted (inspired by zeal in the cause) whatever he wanted, and cooked it as he fancied. If ever there was a device better suited than another for promoting a system of false and calumnious

[1] We have to acknowledge the kindness of the Synod of Galloway, of the Presbytery of Wigtown, and of the Kirk-Sessions of Kirkinner, Wigtown, and Penninghame, in affording us the free use of their respective records.

history, it was this universal and hasty raking of all the common
sewers of fanaticism for the discovery of some unknown quantity of
sufferings.'[1]

Mr. Napier may think it very wicked in the Church of Scotland to
have entertained the idea of preserving in history any record of the
sad times prior to the Revolution in 1688; and certainly it must be
allowed, that had they, out of charity, taken no account of the sufferings of these times, their charity would indeed have 'covered a multitude of sins.'   But whether it was from want of charity, or from love
of truth, the fact is, that the Church of Scotland, just about twenty
years after the Revolution of 1688, did form the design of writing the
history of the Restoration period, and did adopt the plan of collecting
materials through the agency of her own judicatories.   This plan was
at least a natural one; and if the parties employed in it may be
supposed to have looked at events, still recent, through their strong
prejudices, and to have given them the colour of their own still heated
blood, no one need wonder; especially when it is seen that Mr. Napier
himself (who is probably no great sufferer by the Revolution settle-
ment, and who, it is to be hoped, will long enjoy the protection and
patronage of the reigning dynasty) cannot, from his point of view, look
back to these times, over the intervening ages, without being excited
to no ordinary warmth of expression, and manifesting at least a full
share of that prejudice from which no reader or writer of history is
altogether free.   At all events, the plan of collecting materials for the
projected history through the instrumentality of the church courts, was
so far favourable to the cause of truth that it gave very full publicity
to what was being done.   These courts were open to the public, and
the injunction to take up accounts of the sufferings in the late times
was renewed at almost every meeting of synod and presbytery for
several years.[2]   If the church was bent on gathering up false and
calumnious statements, they at least gave all men notice to watch
their proceedings.

The parochial collectors, too—the minister and elders met and
constituted in session—gave their guarantee for the truth of the facts
which they recorded, and took upon themselves the responsibility of
answering any who might challenge them; and they drew up their
minutes with the knowledge that they would be submitted to the
higher courts, and so brought under the eyes of many whose knowledge of the events recorded would enable them easily to detect any
falsehood.   It must be remembered also that these parochial courts of
the church have by statute a jurisdiction allotted to them; and down
to a recent date their records were the sole legal vouchers of a most
important set of facts—the births and marriages that took place in
their respective parishes.   These records may be defective (just be-

---

[1] *Case for the Crown*, p. 96.

[2] The taking up accounts of the sufferings was before the Synod of Galloway ten times
between 1708 and 1713; and before the Presbytery of Wigtown fifty-nine times between
1708 and 1716.

cause sessions had no power to compel a man to register his marriage or his child's birth), but false statements or intentional inaccuracies cannot be imputed to them. When, therefore, a man can appeal to one of these old records in proof of his ancestor's marriage, and of his own legitimate descent, he produces evidence which no judge in the kingdom can refuse to receive. Like other courts, kirk-sessions have erred in their judgments; but that they could assert *that* to be a fact, of which they had no certain knowledge, or which they knew to be altogether false, is what no one who knows anything of the men who have in all times composed the eldership of the Church of Scotland will readily believe. Even one honest man in a kirk-session would effectually prevent any such fraud; for he would feel himself constrained to enter his dissent, and to bring the matter under review of the superior court.

In order, however, to see the full force of this branch of the proof of the Wigtown martyrdom, it will be necessary to follow the steps taken by the church courts in collecting the accounts of the sufferings in their bounds; to mark who were the men that gave their testimony on this matter, when and where they lived (so far as can be ascertained), and what opportunity they had of knowing the truth of what they have recorded. It will be necessary, too, to notice the security given for their recording a true statement, not only by their character and position, but also by the circumstances in which they gave their testimony. It must be noticed, besides, who were the men that *accepted their testimony*,—those who, living in the neighbourhood, had undoubted knowledge of what took place in 1685. For while such of them as were friends of the Church of Scotland would not have allowed a notoriously false statement to go into print, those on the other side would have given the alarm, had any manifest slander against the late Government been attempted, and the *Case for the Crown* would then have appeared.

(1.) *Presbytery and Synod.*

The order of the Church of Scotland to collect accounts of the sufferings for religion in the late times of persecution, seems to have been issued in 1708, just twenty years after the Revolution; for, in the minute of the Presbytery of Wigtown, dated 10th February 1708, appears the first reference to the subject: 'The presbytery being desired, by a letter from the Commission, to bring in ane account of the sufferings of the late tymes upon account of religion, within their bounds, they appoint the several brethren to be at pains to inquire into this, and make report to their next.' Nothing being effectually done in the matter, the appointment is renewed at several subsequent meetings of presbytery, and 'at that held on 13th July the brethren are recommended to be at more pains to get their accounts 'sufficiently attested.'

In the same year 1708, on the 19th October, the Synod of Galloway met at Wigtown; and in their minute of that date is given their first recommendation to the several presbyteries in their bounds regarding this matter :—

'The synod, considering that there is a design of writing a historie of the sufferings of this church under Episcopacie in the late tymes, did therefore recommend to the several presbyteries to get ane exact account of the sufferings of the late tymes in their bounds, and to bring them to next synod; and appoints Messrs. William Clark of Twynholm (ordained 1693), and William Falconer of Kelton (ord. 1695), to call for an account of these sufferings from the Presbytery of Kirkcudbright; and Messrs. Thomas Campbell of Monygaff (ord. 1699), and Thomas Ker of Wigtown (ord. 1701), for the Presbytery of Wigtown; and Messrs. Robert Colvill, Old Luce (ord. 1698), and Walter Laurie, Stranraer (ord. 1695), for the Presbytery of Stranraer.'[1]

The synod received reports on this subject, and renewed their instructions to the several presbyteries at their subsequent meetings in 1709–10; and at their meeting, 17th October 1710, another letter from the Commission of the General Assembly is laid before them, and, in compliance with its recommendation, the synod enjoined the presbyteries 'to be diligent in getting up these accounts,' and 'to send them *quam primum* to the Procurator for the Church.'

In compliance with the above order, the Presbytery of Wigtown reported to the synod, which met at Wigtown 21st April 1713, 'that Mr. Rowan has sent in what account could be got of the sufferings of the late times from the session of Penninghame, to the Procurator for the Church.'[2]

It does not appear that any of the presbyteries sent their accounts of the sufferings in their bounds through the synod; still it cannot be doubted (seeing that the synod met at Wigtown on eight several occasions, when the subject of the sufferings was before them) that it was well known to all the members what account was given of the Wigtown suffering, and whether that account was true or not; and it is only on the supposition that the account given was true, that it is possible to explain the fact, that of the men who composed the synod, no one complained of that which, had it been untrue, would have been alike discreditable to themselves, and injurious to the church.[3]

[1] At this meeting of synod all the ministers of the Presbytery of Wigtown, ten in number, were present,—also an elder from each parish; nine ministers and four elders from Kirkcudbright; eight ministers and two elders from Stranraer; one elder, as correspondent, from the Synod of Glasgow and Ayr.

[2] The Penninghame Session minute, as will be shown, was submitted to the presbytery on 27th February 1711, before it was sent to Edinburgh.

[3] We give a few of the names of elders present in the synod when the subject of 'the sufferings' was under consideration, who could not be ignorant of the fate of the two women: *John Lafries*, bailie of Wigtown in 1689 (on the Roll of Synod in 1692); *Thomas M'Clellan*, tenant of Carslae, in the parish of Wigtown (on the Roll of Synod in 1694); *Henry Donaldson*, bailie of Whithorn (on the Roll of Synod in 1690); *William Wilson*, bailie of Stranraer. Of proprietors of land in the district, some in the neighbourhood of Wigtown: *John M'Culloch* of Barholm, *Andrew Heron* of Bargallie, *Alexander Halliday* of Mark, *Samuel M'Dowall* of Glen, *The Laird of Cardoness*, *Robert Gordon* of Garrarie (on the Synod Roll in 1694), *Gordon* of Achendolly, *Gordon* of Largmore (on the Synod Roll in 1694), *John Martin* of Airies, *George Martin* of Cutcloy, *Alexander*

The proceedings of the Presbytery of Wigtown, acting under the injunctions of the synod, may now be looked into. On the 1st March 1709, there were laid before the presbytery the minutes of synod, which, *inter alia*, appoint ' Messrs. Thomas Campbell (of Monigaff) and Ker (of Wigtown) to be at pains to collect accounts of the sufferings of the late times in every parish.' The fact that Mr. Ker, minister of Wigtown, was appointed to this duty, is not irrelevant, and may be kept in mind; for though the task laid upon the two brethren was not accomplished by them, Mr. Ker was probably led to make particular inquiry into the case of the two women who had been condemned to be drowned at Wigtown in 1685. It would seem, however, that the duty of collecting the sufferings in ' every parish' was too much for the two brethren; for though their appointment is renewed on the 19th May 1709, the presbytery, at their next meeting (19th July), adopted what was doubtless a better plan : ' The presbytery appoint *each session* to bring ane account of the sufferings in the several parishes to the next [meeting].' The parochial collectors thus appointed do not seem to deserve the praise for ' *zeal* ' which Mr. Napier bestows on them; for though the appointment is renewed, sometimes peremptorily, at every monthly meeting of presbytery, from July 1709 to January 1711, at the latter date not even one of the sessions had given in ' ane account of the sufferings.' It must be allowed that their ' zeal ' did not outrun their discretion. The first statements given in were the two important ones—those of Kirkinner and of Penninghame, both on the 27th February 1711. But before looking at the minute of that date, attention must first be given to the proceedings of these two kirk-sessions.

(2.) *Kirk-Session of Kirkinner.*

The Kirk-Session of Kirkinner took up the subject of the sufferings in their parish, for the first time, on the 15th January 1710; and from that date till the 15th April 1711, when their statement of sufferings was ordered to be recorded in their minutes, it appears that they had this matter before them at many of their meetings. The minute of the 15th April 1711 is as follows :—

' *Post preces* sederunt all the members except John M'Culloch, William Hanna, and John Martin, younger in Airles.' *Inter alia*, ' The minister gave in the account of the sufferings of honest godly people in the late times, which was read, and is as follows: Margaret Laughlison, of known integrity and piety from her youth, aged about 80, widow of John Milliken, wright in Drumjargan, was, in or

---

Martin, younger of Cutcloy, *Sir Charles Hay* of Park (on the Roll of Commissioners of Supply in 1685 ; on the Synod Roll in 1694), *John Blair* of Dunskey (on the Roll of Synod in 1691), *Robert M'Dowall* of Logan, *Patrick M'Dowall* of Culgroat ; and *Sir James Agnew* of Lochnaw, the hereditary sheriff of Wigtownshire, who was of age to remember the events of 1685 ; for he was married in 1683, and we have seen that in 1684 he appeared at Wigtown to take the test. He was a member of synod on two occasions when ' the sufferings' were under consideration, viz. 18th October 1709, and 18th April 1710.

about the year of God 1685, in her own house, taken off her knees in prayer, and carried immediately to prison, and from one prison to another, without the benefit of light to read the Scriptures; was barbarously treated by dragoons, who were ·sent to carry her from Mahirmore to Wigtown; and being sentenced by Sir Robert Grier, of Lagg, to be drowned at a stake within the flood-mark just below the town of Wigtown, for conventicle keeping and alleged rebellion, was, according to the said sentence, fixed to the stake till the tide made, and held down within the water by one of the town-officers by his halbert at her throat till she died.'

After narrating *twelve* other cases of suffering, in forms of banishment, imprisonment, fining, etc., the minute concludes:—

' The which particulars aforesaid being read, they, partly from credible information, partly from their own personal knowledge, do believe the said informations to be matters of fact, and appoint the same to be recorded in their session-book *ad futuram rei memoriam,* and the clerk to give extract to the Presbytery of Wigtown according to appointment. Sederunt closed with prayer.'[1]

What has Mr. Napier got to say as to this narrative ? ' Margaret Wilson, the prima donna of that water opera, is *not there.* This is not Wodrow's story, not Lord Macaulay's story, not the story that the world has.' The minister of Kirkinner, in this ' the very Hamlet of our martyrologies,' has been so stupid ' as to *omit the part of Ophelia.'* [2]

It does not affect the credibility of the Kirkinner minute that it has not been written in dramatic form; and as to Margaret Wilson not being mentioned in it, that is easily explained. Each session was to record the sufferings of their own parishioners; and as Margaret Wilson did not belong to Kirkinner, she is not mentioned in the account from that parish. The session of Penninghame, it is true, took a different course, and mentioned *both* women, evidently because both were condemned and executed together. But, at the same time, they state that Margaret Lauchlison belonged to Kirkinner. This and

[1] It will be noticed that this minute was laid before the presbytery before it was for the last time read in the session and ordered to be recorded. That is an irregularity; but it will not be imagined that the minute given to the presbytery was a different one from that approved by the session.

Besides *Margaret Lauchlison,* several others in the session list of sufferers are marked *disorderly* in Mr. Symson's list, viz. : *William Sprott,* in Clutog, who was banished and died at sea ; *Alexander Vans,* laird of Barwhannie (afterwards of Barnbarroch), and his wife, *Margaret Maxwell,* who were ' frequently harassed, processed, and fined ;' also their *servitrix, Margaret Maxwell,* who ' was imprisoned at Wigtown about the year 1685, and scourged there three several times by the hand of the common hangman, and afterwards carried prisoner to Glasgow in order to banishment.'

It is a remarkable coincidence that this Margaret Maxwell should have been one of the authorities of Patrick Walker,—who figures so prominently in Mr. Napier's title-page,— for his account of the martyrdom. He tells us that she lived latterly in Borrowstounness, when he was acquainted with her, and that she told him that she had been a fellow-prisoner of Margaret Lauchlison and Margaret Wilson when they were condemned. Of course, Walker would know nothing of her having been pricked down as disorderly by Symson in his list in October 1684, nor of the corroboration of her story which was contained in the Kirkinner Session minutes. And yet, in these two documents, we find the strongest corroboration of the truth of his informant's testimony.

[2] *Case for the Crown,* p. 98.

F

other differences between the two minutes show that there was no
collusion, and that each session gave its statement without concert
with the other.

The Kirkinner minute mentions only one of the judges—Sir
Robert Grierson. He *was* one of the judges ; and the elders of Kirkinner may well be excused for not knowing who were the other members of a roving Commission of Justiciary, most of whom were strangers.
It is just what may be expected in such a case, that though the main
facts will be remembered, circumstantial details will not be retained,
—perhaps not even noticed at first. How few of the inhabitants of
Edinburgh could tell, from recollection, who were the judges in the
trial of *Burke* and *Hare,* who was counsel for the Crown, who defended the prisoners, or who was the magistrate who saw the sentence
executed ! But no one will fail to remember the nature of the crime,
the fact that one of the prisoners, Hare, was accepted as a witness for
the Crown, and escaped punishment, and that the other was executed.

This session states that their aged parishioner was sentenced 'for
conventicle keeping and alleged rebellion.' This Mr. Napier denies,
and states that she was sentenced 'for refusing to take the oath of
abjuration.' No doubt, refusing to swear this oath was the *immediate*
ground of her sentence ; but was not alleged rebellion in the form of
conventicle keeping the remoter cause ? She was not surely caught
hold of, and dragged into a court of justice, and condemned to die for
not abjuring rebellion, though no act of rebellion had been alleged
against her. Mr. Napier further charges 'this minister and his session'
with ignorance of 'the *proved* facts of the petition and *pardon.*' They
might have known· that there was a petition, and they might have
known (as the Penninghame Session knew) that compliance with the
Government's terms would have stopped the execution, even at the
last hour, which implies knowledge of a reprieve; but certainly they
did not know of the *pardon* as a *proved fact.* Mr. Napier has the
distinction of being the first to know of the *pardon* as a proved fact ;
and as he has attained to that knowledge by a logical process pecu-
liarly his own, he might have viewed the ignorance of this session
with a more charitable eye, and should not have accused them of
' having solemnly attested for truth, *in perpetuam rei memoriam,* and
sealed with prayer *an abominable falsehood.*'[1]

'What manner of man,' says Mr. Napier, 'this minister was, and
what manner of men practically composed this parochial kirk-session,
or really had to do with this rude entry, no man alive can tell, though
some may guess.'[2] Before venturing to *guess* as he has done, Mr.
Napier had better have made further inquiry. He takes credit for
bringing to light the entry in the Kirkinner record, which had

[1] *Case for the Crown,* p. 98. A Scotch sheriff ought to know that all meetings of
church courts, even kirk-sessions, are begun and ended with prayer, and that unless thus
constituted, they have no legal existence.

[2] *Case for the Crown,* p. 98.

'hitherto remained entirely latent;' so he must have had access to the minute-book. And yet he did not think it necessary to inquire who were the men who sanctioned the minute; how many of them there were; and whether, from the dates of their ordination, they were living in Kirkinner in 1685, and were then old enough to remember a fact in their parochial history so remarkable as the putting to death, by drowning, of a fellow-parishioner. These, one would think, are matters worth looking into, by any one really anxious to know the truth of the fact in question. The information which Mr. Napier has thought it unnecessary to give, shall now be supplied.

As has been shown above, the *sederunt* of the Kirkinner Session, on the 15th April 1711, included *all* the members, except three whose names are given; so, from the minutes of 15th October 1710 and 1st July 1711, where all the members of session are named, it is an easy matter to see who were actually present when the minute of sufferings was adopted and ordered to be recorded. The session at this time consisted of *fourteen* members, and *eleven* of these were present at the attestation of the completed minute. The other three were repeatedly present at other meetings, when the same subject was under consideration.

The following were the members present, viz. :—

1. *Mr. William Campbell*, ordained minister of Kirkinner[1] in 1702, and died in 1742. The presbytery minutes show that he was a licentiate of the Presbytery of Wigtown, and that he brought testimonials from the Presbytery of Stranraer. A writer in the *Dumfries Courier*, in a review of our first edition, states that he was a son of the minister of Stonykirk, in that presbytery,—a Wigtownshire man, who must have heard the story of the Wigtown women in his boyhood.

2. *William M'Haffie*, in Kildarroch. He was an elder in Kirkinner when Mr. Campbell came to the parish. When ordained is not known, as the minute-book goes back only to 1702; but, as appears from Mr. Andrew Symson's list, he was living at Kildarroch in 1684, the year before the martyrdom. What better testimony, as regard means of information, could we have than that of a man who we know was living in the parish of Kirkinner at the time of the event in question?

3. *Gilbert Milroy* (residence or designation not given). He was a member of session before 1702.

4. *George Dun* (residence or designation not given). He was an elder in Kirkinner before 1698, at which date his name is on the roll of the synod. He was probably a son of Alexander Dun in Camford, formerly an elder in Kirkinner.

5. *John Martin* of Little Aires. The minute-book shows that he

---

[1] The parish of Kirkinner lies immediately south from that of Wigtown, from which it is separated by the Blednoch. The church is somewhat more than two miles from the Blednoch, and about three miles from the town of Wigtown. Drumjargan is about the same distance; and the residences of the elders are from three to five miles from Wigtown.

was ordained an elder in Kirkinner in 1703. He was an heritor in the parish; he held the sheriff's commission as parish magistrate; and he was regularly sent up as a representative to the General Assembly from 1710 to 1725. The Kirkinner minute of sufferings states that Andrew Martin of Little Aires (probably John's father) was declared rebel for going to Bothwell; so that it is not to be wondered at that no male above twelve years old of the name of Martin appears' in Mr. Symson's list as residing at Little Aires in 1684. But John Martin, ordained in 1703, was doubtless old enough in 1685 to remember the sufferings of that year.[1] His testimony, therefore, we must receive as that of a man of known position, character, and intelligence.

6. *Alexander Martin*, younger of Cutloi (or Cutloy), in the parish of Whithorn. He was at this time probably the tenant of Mickle Aires, in Kirkinner, as he represents the proprietor, Henry Hathorn, at parish meetings. He was ordained an elder in Kirkinner in 1703. His tombstone, still in the churchyard of Whithorn, shows that he ' departed this life the 28th day of July 1715, aged 42.' He was consequently born in 1673, and was about *twelve* years of age at the time of the martyrdom. At that time he lived in the parish of Whithorn with his father, George Martin, also an elder of the church, whose name appears on the roll of the Synod of Galloway on the 16th October 1711,—one of the times when the synod called on presbyteries to report their diligence in collecting an account of the sufferings.[2] It is impossible in such circumstances to suppose Alexander Martin ignorant of the fact in question. His own recollections, aided by those of his father, render his testimony all that could be desired in such a case. He, too, was a man much respected in his day, as a metrical tribute on his tombstone shows.

7. *John Martin*, elder in Airles. He was ordained in 1705; and if, as may be presumed, the father of John Martin, younger in Airles, who was ordained at the same time, he was surely of age in 1685 to testify to what then took place. There is the name John Martin in Mr. Symson's list; but as the residence given is different, it is impossible to say that it is the name of the elder.

[1] It may be here mentioned, once for all, especially for the benefit of those who are not intimately acquainted with the laws and procedure of the Scotch Church, that while it is competent to ordain a man an elder at 21, it is rarely, if ever, done at this early age. Though in the case of an heritor, or an heritor's eldest son,—as, for example, in No. 6, Mr. Martin, younger of Cutcloy,—ordination sometimes took place at 30 or even under, it may be stated, as a general rule, that few were ordained under 30 to 40. In Penninghame it will be seen that William Douglas was 39 when he was ordained, James M'Geoch 37, and Thomas Wilson 50. It is clear, therefore, that the elders who were present at the meetings of synod from 1708 to 1713 (*vide* pp. 79, 80)—many of whom had been ordained before 1694—and the elders of Kirkinner who were ordained previous to 1702, must all have been old enough in 1685 to have had a perfect knowledge of the events that took place in the district in that year.

[2] That the Martins were living on their property (which is fifteen miles from Wigtown) in the end of 1684, is proved by the Whithorn list. The name of Alexander is not in the list, he being then something *under* twelve years.

8. *John M'Dowall*, in Ballaird. He was ordained in 1705. There are two of that name in Mr. Symson's list, but neither of them residing at Ballaird.

9. *John Kirkpatrick*, chamberlain to Basil Hamilton of Baldoon. Ordained in 1707. He came from Edinburgh, and cannot have had personal knowledge of the fact in question, but was doubtless satisfied of its truth on the testimony of others.

10. *Robert Heron*, in Barglass. Admitted an elder in Kirkinner in 1710, having been previously an elder in the neighbouring parish of Mochrum. The name Robert Heron appears on the roll of the synod 20th April 1697; and on 21st October 1701 the same name occurs as elder from Mochrum. One who was an elder in 1697 in an adjoining parish, may be supposed to have had some knowledge of what took place at Wigtown in 1685.

11. *Andrew Gray, ordained Deacon in* 1705.

The three members of session who were absent on the 15th April when the minute of sufferings was finally attested, but who were present at other meetings when it was under consideration, and no doubt agreed to all that was contained in it, were—

1. *John M'Culloch*, who was ordained an elder before 1702, the date at which the minute-book commences.

2. *William Hanna*, also one of the old elders. This name appears in Mr. Symson's list as residing at Blairshinnoch in the end of 1684.

3. *John Martin*, younger in Airles, ordained in 1705.[1]

It was not, then, a matter of *tradition* which these elders attested and recorded as the suffering of Margaret Lauchlison, but a fact which had taken place within the remembrance of the youngest of them, of which most of them must have had personal knowledge, and of which some of them may have been eye-witnesses. No one, therefore, need wonder why ' no other or more precise record of the facts is referred to—no formal precognition is recorded, or pretended to have been taken—no certificate or information by an eye-witness is pretended to be forthcoming.'[2] This kirk-session was recording a remarkable parochial event, which had taken place in their own day, and they did not think it necessary to corroborate their own statement by the testimony of others. And it ought to be remarked, that they were not recording a statement that was to remain ' latent' for a century and a half, but one that was to be immediately submitted to the superior church courts, and forthwith published. It is impossible to conceive that these men were ignorant of what was really the fate of their parishioner. Did they then solemnly record the story of her martyrdom, *knowing it to be false*, and give it in to be read in the Presbytery of Wigtown, and in the hearing of the people of Wigtown, who knew the true story? No degree of moral worthlessness could account for such conduct. It would betoken, besides, such extreme folly, that no body of men ever could be guilty of it.

[1] Alexander Vans of Barnbarroch (who was one of the persecuted) was an elder in Kirkinner, but had recently died.   [2] *Case for the Crown*, p. 99.

Mr. Napier, in words above quoted, complains that no precognition was taken, nor eye-witnesses examined. He has shown how he would have estimated such testimony had it been taken. There was living in the parish of Kirkinner, so late as 1718, Elizabeth Milliken, daughter of Margaret Lauchlison. She was living in Kirkinner a married woman in 1685; for not only are she and her husband mentioned among the sufferers, in the session minute, but their names are given in Mr. Symson's list. Indeed, we learn further from this list, that Margaret Lauchlison was, in the end of 1684, living with them in their house at Drumjargan. We might therefore expect, as a matter of course, that the daughter would have known *for certain* what had become of her mother, who had been residing with her in 1685, who had been taken out of her house by soldiers, and who had been publicly tried and condemned in the town of Wigtown, about three miles distant. *She* must have known, surely, whether her mother took the oath, was liberated, and came back to Drumjargan, or whether she really was drowned in the Blednoch. And though the session did not think it necessary to take her formal precognition, a circumstance occurred seven years afterwards, in 1718, which led to her testimony being recorded. Wodrow—who has represented Provost Coltron as one of the judges in the trial, though he had no authority in the minutes of either kirk-session for doing so—had heard that Elizabeth Milliken had a remarkable dream, in which her mother appeared to her, and told her to warn the Provost of his approaching end. Wodrow wrote to Mr. Campbell, minister of Kirkinner, to make inquiry into this matter; and Mr. Campbell's letter to Wodrow, giving an account of his conversation with Elizabeth Milliken, is preserved. She told Mr. Campbell that she dreamed 'that her mother, Margaret Lauchlison, came to her at the cross of Wigtown, with the garb, gesture, and countenance that she had five minutes before she was drowned in Blednoch, etc.' This surely implies that *she believed that her mother was put to death by drowning, and that she had seen her led forth to execution.* As to her believing that Provost Coltron was one of those concerned in her mother's death, on that point she might be mistaken; but regarding her mother's fate, it is impossible to conceive that she was.

What has Mr. Napier to say regarding the testimony of this *eye-witness?* 'That her mother was drowned as described in the Kirkinner session-book of 1711, is a hallucination or confusion which she might very easily imbibe from her minister, who was assuming the fact, and much interested to have it embellished as a fact.'[1] So it would seem that this minister of Kirkinner, though (in Mr. Napier's judgment) very deficient in moral qualities, was highly gifted in other respects,—was indeed a wizard of no ordinary powers, who could make people believe in things as facts which were contrary to their own personal knowledge,—who in this case made a woman believe, and even *declare*, that she had seen her mother carried away to execution,

[1] *Case for the Crown*, p. 114.

though no such thing ever happened. One who can believe in parish ministers being thus gifted, need not boggle at a ghost. But the fact is, the ghost in this instance is an invention of the author of the *Case for the Crown.* This woman did not say she had seen a ghost, but merely that she had dreamed of her dead mother; which was nothing very remarkable. She thought there was something in her dream; and Wodrow and Mr. Campbell seem to have thought the matter worth inquiring into, which was fortunate for our argument, as otherwise we might not have got this daughter's testimony as to her mother's execution. As the matter stands, her statement to Mr. Campbell must be regarded as such a testimony by all who believe this minister incapable of producing a 'hallucination' or *inventing* a statement, which must have been useless in his day, though it is of value in ours.

(3.) *Kirk-Session of Penninghame.*

The proceedings of the Kirk-Session of Penninghame may now be looked into. This kirk-session, it appears, with the same unanimity as their brethren at Kirkinner, certify the main fact in question; but still with such difference in circumstantial details, as to show that there was no concert between them. There are thus furnished separate proofs of the same fact, by two sets of independent witnesses.

The subject of the 'sufferings' is before the session of Penninghame, for the first time, on the 15th February 1711, on which occasion the minister, Mr. Rowan, 'presented a collection of the sufferings given up to him by the persons best acquainted with them, which, being read, the session informs of several material things that are wanting, and orders them to be inserted and presented.'[1] Accordingly, on the 19th February 1711 (this, and not 25th February, is the date in the minute-book), it is recorded : 'The particulars that were wanting in the account of the sufferings of the people under the late Prelacy being insert in the former account, all was produced and read, the tenor whereof follows.' The minute is a long one, and contains the names of *twenty-nine* persons connected with the parish, who had been subjected to suffering in various forms. The part of the minute relating to the Wilson family is as follows :—

'Gilbert Wilson of Glenvernock, in Castlestewart's land, being a man to ane excesse conform to the guise of the tymes, and his wife without challenge for her religion, in good condition as to worldly things, with a great stock on a large ground (fitt to be a prey), was harassed for his childrene who would not conform. They being required to take the test, and hear the curates, refused both; were searched for, fled, and lived in the wild mountains, bogs, and caves. Their parents were charged, on their highest peril, that they should neither harbour them, speak to them, supplie them, nor see them; and the country people were obliged by the terror of the law, to.pursue them, as well as the soldiers, with hue and cry.

'In February 1685, Thomas Wilson, of sixteen years of age, Margaret Wilson of eighteen years, Agnes Wilson of thirteen years, children of the said Gilbert,— the said Thomas keeping the mountains, his two sisters Margaret and Agnes went

---

[1] There can be no doubt that so important a case as that of the Wilsons was in the first scroll submitted to the session, and was consequently read at *both* meetings.

secretly to Wigtown to see some friends, were there discovered, taken prisoners, and instantly thrust into the thieves hole as the greatest malefactors; whence they were some tymes brought up to the tolbooth, after a considerable tyme's imprisonment, where several others were prisoners for the like cause, particularly one Margaret M'Lachland of Kirkinner paroch, a woman of sixty-three years of age.

'After their imprisonment for some considerable tyme, Mr. David Graham, sheriff, the Laird of Lagg, Major Winram, Captain Strachan, called ane assize, indicted these three women, viz. Margaret M'Lachlan, Margaret Wilson, Agnes Wilson, to be guilty of the Rebellion at Bothwell-bridge, Airds Mosse, twenty field conventicles, and twenty house conventicles. Yet it was well known that none of these women ever were within twenty miles of Bothwell or Airds Mosse; and Agnes Wilson, being eight years of age at the time of Airds Mosse, could not be deep in rebellion then, nor her sister of thirteen years of age, and twelve years at Bothwell-bridge its tyme. The assize did sitt, and brought them in guilty, and these judges sentenced them *to be tyed to palisados fixed in the sand, within the flood-mark, and there to stand till the flood overflowed them, and drowned them.*

'They received their sentence without the least discouragement, with a composed smiling countenance, judging it their honour to suffer for Christ's truth, that He is alone King and Head of his Church. Gilbert Wilson, forsaid, got his youngest daughter, Agnes Wilson, out of prison, upon his bond of ane hundreth pounds sterling, to produce her when called for, after the sentence of death past against her; but was obliged to go to Edinburgh for this before it could be obtained. The tyme they were in prison no means were unessayed with Margaret Wilson to persuade her to take the oath of abjuration, and hear the curates, with threatenings and flattery, but without any success.

'Upon the eleventh day of May 1685, these two women, Margaret M'Lachland and Margaret Wilson, were brought forth to execution. They did put the old woman first into the water, and when the water was overflowing her, they asked Margaret Wilson what she thought of her in that case? She answered, What do I see but Christ wrestling there? Think ye that we are sufferers? No, it is Christ in us, for He sends none a warfare on their own charges. Margaret Wilson sang Psalm xxv. from the 7th verse, read the eighth chapter of the Epistle to the Romans, and did pray, and then the water covered her. But before her breath was quite gone, they pulled her up, and held her till she could speak, and then asked her if she would pray for the King. She answered that she wished the salvation of all men, but the damnation of none. Some of her relations being on the place, cried out, She is willing to conform, being desirous to save her life at any rate. Upon which Major Winram offered the oath of abjuration to her, either to swear it, or return to the waters. She refused it, saying, " I will not. I am one of Christ's children, let me go." And then they returned her into the water, where she finished her warfare, being a virgin martyr of eighteen years of age, suffering death for her refusing to swear the oath of abjuration and hear the curates.

'The said Gilbert Wilson was fined for the opinion of his children, harassed with frequent quarterings of souldiers upon him, sometymes ane hundreth men at ance, who lived at discretion on his goods, and that for several years together; and his frequent attendance in the courts at Wigtown almost every week, at thirteen miles distance, for three years tyme; riding to Edinburgh on these accounts, so that his losses could not be reckoned, and estimat (without doubt) not within five thousand merks: yet for no principle or action of his own, and died in great poverty lately a few years hence: his wife, a very aged woman, lives upon the charity of friends: his son Thomas lived to bear arms under King William in Flanders, and the castle of Edinburgh; but had nothing to enter the ground which they possessed, where he lives to certifie the truth of these things, with many others who knew them too weel.'

The attestation, applicable not to this case merely, but to *all* the cases recorded in the minute, is in the following terms:—

'The session having considered the above particulars, and having certain knowledge of the truth of most part of them from their own sufferings,[1] and eye-witnesses of the foresaid sufferings of others, which several of this session declares, and from certain information of others in the very tyme and place they were acted in, and many living that have all these things fresh in their memory, except of those things concerning Gilbert Milroy,[2] the truth whereof they think there is no ground to doubt of—they do attest the same, and orders ane extract to be given in their name to the presbytery, to transmitt to superior judicatories. Sederunt closed with prayer.'

The Penninghame minute-book shows who were the men who at that time composed the kirk-session, where they lived, when they were ordained; and Mr. Colhoun's list of the parishioners, dated 29th September 1684, will make it a matter of perfect certainty regarding a number of them, that, being resident in Penninghame at the time of the event in question, they must have had the most perfect knowledge of it. The session, at the time when the minute in question was agreed to, was as follows:—

1. *Mr. Robert Rowan*, minister of Penninghame.[3] He was settled in this parish on the 4th November 1696, eleven years after the martyrdom, and died in 1714, at the age of 55.

2. *John M'Caul*, in Corsbie. He was ordained by Mr. Thomas Cobham before 1696. The minute states that, having been at Bothwell, he was taken and imprisoned for a quarter of a year at Dumfries; but, on his landlord, Castle-Stewart, giving Claverhouse a bond of a thousand merks for his compearance when called, he was liberated. His son, John M'Caul, minister of Whithorn from 1712 to 1741, was born (as his tombstone shows) in 1685, the year of the martyrdom. Mr. Colhoun's list shows that John M'Caul (spelled M'Cawell) was living at Corsbie in the end of 1684.

3. *John Martin*, in Glenvogie. He was ordained before 1696, and was also a sufferer, as is stated in the minute. He was not present at either of the meetings when the minute was read. His wife and son are in Mr. Colhoun's list, but his name is not there. In this circumstance we have a confirmation of his own 'suffering,' as stated in the minute. He was obliged to abscond. But though a fugitive at the time, he doubtless knew all that befel his near neighbours the Wilsons.

4. *John Heron*, in Grange of Cree, which is between two and three miles from Wigtown. He also was ordained before 1696. In the end of 1684, as Mr. Colhoun's list shows, he was living at Grange of Cree, with his father, James Heron.

5. *Alexander M'Gill*, in Barvenan. He was ordained deacon before

---

[1] Several of the members of session were sufferers.

[2] Gilbert Milroy was banished, sold as a slave in Jamaica, had returned, and was then an elder in the neighbouring parish of Kirkcowan.

[3] The *old* church of Penninghame was about four miles north from Wigtown. The parishes of Penninghame and Kirkinner almost encircle that of Wigtown. The former is a large parish, the upper part of it being mostly pastoral, while the lower comes within two miles of Wigtown.

1696, and elder in 1700. He was, according to Mr. Colhoun's list, living at Barvenan in the end of 1684.

6. *Thomas M'Caw*, in Challoch; ordained deacon before 1696, and elder in 1707. This name does not occur in Mr. Colhoun's list.

7. *John M'Keand*, in Balsalloch; ordained in 1700. He was not present when the minute was read. In Mr. Colhoun's list there are two of this name (spelled M'Kaine) resident at Balsalloch.

8. *William Douglas*, in Balsalloch. He was ordained deacon in 1700, and elder in 1707. His tombstone, in the old churchyard of Penninghame, shows that he 'died the 14th Oct. 1745, aged 77.' He was consequently seventeen years of age at the date of the martyrdom. He does not appear to have been resident in Penninghame in 1684, as his name does not occur in Mr. Colhoun's list.

9. *James M'Geoch*, in Barwhirran. He was ordained in 1704. His tombstone, in the old churchyard of Penninghame, shows that he 'died 1714, aged 47.' He was consequently eighteen years of age in 1685. Mr. Colhoun's list shows, that in the end of 1684 he was living at Barwhirran with his father, Robert M'Geoch.

10. *John M'Clelland*, bailie in Newton-Stewart. He was admitted in 1704, having been previously an elder in the neighbouring parish of Monigaff.

11. *Alexander M'Clingan*, in Barachan. He was ordained an elder 1704, and lived till 1721. This is the same person whose name occurs in the minute as having been himself one of those belonging to Penninghame who suffered in the late times, and whose wife (Margaret M'Lurg), as has been stated above, was sentenced to banishment by the Commission at Wigtown in 1684 for 'converse' with him. That Alex. M'Clingan, ordained elder in 1704, is the same person as the 'sufferer' in the minute, and not another of the same name, is proved by a session minute, dated April 23, 1710, in which it appears that Alex. M'Clingan, elder, asks the session to grant him a certificate of his inability to attend the Justiciary Court at Ayr, 'through age and infirmity, contracted by his distresses, which he, under the late persecution by Prelacy, endured.' No one can doubt that he, though a fugitive in 1685, was well informed as to the sufferings in Penninghame at that time, and could not but know what was the fate of Margaret Wilson. In 1684 his residence was at *Thrive*, in Penninghame. His wife's name is in Mr. Colhoun's list as resident there; but the minister, when making the list, recollected that the head of the house was a fugitive, and, after having commenced to write his name, had erased it.

12. *Patrick Milroy*, in Glenhapple; ordained in 1707. This name is not in Mr. Colhoun's list.

13. *James M'Millan*, in Fintilloch; ordained in 1707. He was not present when the minute was read, neither does his name occur in Mr. Colhoun's list.[1]

---

[1] It deserves to be noticed, that when Mr. Rowan was settled in 1696, there were then in the session three elders—John Martin, in Glenhapple; Michael M'Taggart, in

It thus appears, that of those who in 1711 constituted the Session of Penninghame, and then certified the martyrdom, about one-half of the number are proved, *by the indisputable evidence of Mr. Colhoun's list*, to have been resident in this parish from before the date of the disputed fact; and therefore their testimony must be allowed to be that of men who could not be mistaken, at least as to the main facts of the recorded statement. Even the other elders, who may not have been resident in Penninghame in 1685, were most probably living in adjoining parishes, and were of age to remember so remarkable an event.

Besides the elders of Penninghame, there were others in the parish who knew, even better than they, the story of Margaret Wilson's fate —her own near relatives. Mr. Rowan could not have been long settled in Penninghame till he would have heard Margaret Wilson's history from the lips of her parents; and *they* surely knew whether she was executed according to her sentence, or whether, being pardoned, she returned to her home. And in 1711, when Mr. Rowan drew up the minute of sufferings, though Gilbert Wilson was dead, his widow was still alive, as was their son Thomas, who had succeeded his father in the farm of Glenvernock. From them, doubtless, the minister received the account of the sufferings of their family, and the minute details of Margaret's cruel death; for he points to Thomas Wilson as his chief authority, when he says that ' he lives to certify the truth of these things.'

It is, no doubt, a very important point in the evidence of the fact in question, that Thomas Wilson, who was sixteen years of age in 1685,—who shared many of his sister's sufferings, and knew, doubtless, what befel her at last,—was living in the parish of Penninghame in 1711, when the session minute was drawn up, and is especially referred to as ready to certify the truth of that part of it which relates to his sister. And lest any may say that the circumstance that Thomas Wilson's name is thus used in the minute is no proof that he was then living in Penninghame to certify anything about the matter, proof will now be given which will put this point beyond contradiction.

A minute of session, May 7, 1704, is as follows:—' They (the session) having unanimously pitched upon Thomas Wilson, in Glenvernoch, as a person fit for the office of an elder, desire the minister to converse with him, and if he can be prevailed with to accept, that his edict may be served, and he ordained with the others.' Subsequent minutes show that, though written to and spoken to by the minister, he could not at that time be induced to join the session. But many years after, he was persuaded to accept the office repeatedly pressed on him; and the minute-book shows that he was ordained an elder in Penninghame, Nov. 1, 1719. From that date his name appears in the

Castle-Stewart ; Thomas M'Keand, in Balsalloch (whose brother John was ordained elder in 1700)—who were ' ordained by Mr. James Carshore in the tyme of Presbytery, before the coming in of Prelacy, in the year 1662.' The first-named of the three died in 1702 ; the other two acted as elders till 1704.

minute-book as a member of the Penninghame Session down to April
1, 1734. It is thus put beyond all doubt, that *twenty-three* years after
the story of Margaret Wilson was recorded in the Penninghame session-
book, and *twelve* years after it was published in Wodrow's *History*,
Thomas Wilson was still living to certify its truth. It may be that
he was never called upon to certify anything regarding his sister's
death, after her story was published, just because no one in his day
ventured to call that fact in question. Mr. Napier has intimated what
value *he* would put on any attestation by this ' Orange rebel:' had he
' actually attested the fate of his sister, as narrated by the martyr-
ologist, it would just come to this, that Thomas Wilson had attested
for truth that which *is proved to be false*, as did the kirk-sessions of
Kirkinner and Penninghame.'[1] It may, however, be pretty confidently
anticipated, that the great majority of thinkers will trust rather to the
testimony of ' Orange rebels ' and ' Presbyterian ministers and elders,'
than to the soundness of Mr. Napier's logical deductions.

(4.) *Presbytery of Wigtown.*

We now return to the Presbytery of Wigtown, in whose minutes
of the 27th February 1711 it is stated that the ministers of Penninghame and Kirkinner gave in the accounts which their kirk-sessions
had sanctioned: 'Messrs. Rowan and William Campbell tabled ane
account of the sufferings within their respective parishes in the late
times. The appointment is renewed upon the rest of the brethren.'
There were present at this meeting the ministers of all the parishes
in the presbytery, except Whithorn, which was vacant, viz.:—1. *Mr.
William Campbell* (moderator), Kirkinner, 1702, †1742, said to be a
son of the minister of Stonykirk, in the county of Wigtown; 2. *Mr.
Robert Rowan*, Penninghame, 1696, †1714; 3. *Mr. Archibald Haddin*,
Sorbie, 1700, †1721; 4. *Mr. Robert Seaton*, Glasserton, 1700, †1744,
aged 80; 5. *Mr. Thomas Ker*, Wigtown, 1701, †1729; 6. *Mr. William
Cooper*, Mochrum, 1701, †1747; 7. *Mr. Samuel Brown*, Kirkmabreck,
1702, †1751, aged 74 (one of the Browns of Barharrow, in the
stewartry of Kirkcudbright); 8. *Mr. James Murdoch*, Kirkcowan,
1700, †1718, aged 51 (he was a native of Balmaclellan, in the stewartry
of Kirkcudbright, and was an elder in that parish when he was
licensed); 9. *Mr. Thomas Campbell* (clerk), Monigaff, 1699, †1744
(said to be a son of the minister of Stonykirk, Wigtownshire).[2]

There were present also at this meeting of presbytery four elders:
—1. *Hugh Dunse*, from Whithorn; 2. *Patrick M'Lurg*, from Monigaff; 3. *George Dun*, from Kirkinner; 4. *John M'Caul*, from Glasserton, son of the Penninghame elder of the same name. He was at this

---

[1] *Case for the Crown*, p. 105.

[2] The dates are taken partly from the presbytery records, and partly from Dr. Hew
Scott's *Fasti Ecclesiæ Scoticanæ*. It is worthy of notice, that both Mr. Brown of Kirkmabreck and Mr. Campbell of Monigaff married sisters or daughters of Patrick Murdoch
of Camboddan. Their wives, therefore, having been born and brought up within a few
miles of Glenvernock, must have known all about the Wilsons.

time residing at Glasserton as domestic chaplain to James, fifth Earl of Galloway, and was afterwards minister of Whithorn from 1712 to 1741.

Did the Presbytery of Wigtown, constituted as stated above, hear the minutes of the two kirk-sessions read, and without dissent receive them, and order them to be transmitted to the Clerk of the General Assembly, to be used as the materials of the forthcoming history? The minute of presbytery above quoted implies this.   The term 'tabled' implies that the papers were read and received; and indeed the reason why these accounts were taken to the presbytery doubtless was, that the presbytery might give them their sanction as statements which they believed to be true.

The records of the presbytery afford ample proof that the accounts of sufferings from the several sessions were read in the presbytery. Thus it is minuted under date 20th November 1711: 'Mr. Robert Seaton left ane account of the sufferings for religion in the late times for the paroch of Glasserton: to be read at the next.'   Accordingly, it is recorded, 18th December following: 'The account of the sufferings of the late times from Glasserton paroch was read, and is to be kept *in retentis* until it be sent to Edinburgh.'   Again, it is minuted under date 26th June 1716: 'This day Mr. Thomas Campbell produced an account of the sufferings of the late times within his parish.   The reading thereof is delayed till the next; as also that from Kirkcowan.' But at next meeting, on 29th July following, the ministers of Kirkcowan and Monigaff being absent, it is minuted that the reading of these accounts is 'delayed till Messrs. Murdoch and Thomas Campbell be present.'   At next meeting (22d August), Mr. Campbell was present, but Mr. Murdoch was absent; so the following is the minute: 'The account of the sufferings within the parish of Monigaff were this day read, which, Mr. Campbell says, are in the records of their session. He is appointed to send them out to Nicol Spence, sub-clerk to the Assembly.   The Presbytery delay the reading of the sufferings in the parish of Kirkcowan till Mr. Murdoch be present.'   At next meeting, when Mr. Murdoch was present, the Kirkcowan minute was read.

It is thus perfectly certain that the presbytery did not order these parochial statements to be forwarded to Edinburgh without looking at them.   They were all formally read in their hearing (the minister of the parish from which each was sent being present to give any explanation required), and then they were ordered to be transmitted to the Clerk of the General Assembly.   Thus the presbytery sanctioned them as statements which they believed to be true.

Some of the members of presbytery, it may be allowed, could have no personal knowledge of the Wigtown 'suffering;' but all of them must have had ample opportunities of conversing with those who did know about it, and could have had no doubt as to the general belief on the subject; and had that belief been different from the statements given in, there must have been some in the presbytery who would have demanded proof of the execution before sanctioning the session minutes, in which it was asserted to be a fact. The unanimity of the presbytery (in which every parish in the bounds was represented) shows that, twenty-six years after the event, the non-drowning theory had not yet found any supporters in Wigtownshire. The absence of any difference of opinion within the presbytery shows that there was no difference of opinion without it, on the point in question.

(5.) *People of Wigtown.*

At the meeting of presbytery where the two minutes were given in and read, there was no doubt a number of the people of Wigtown present. The presbytery is an open court; and at a time when there were neither reporters nor newspapers, it may be supposed that church courts were more generally attended by the public, even than they are now. At that time, too, the presbytery was always opened with public worship and sermon, which the people were expected to attend.[1] Of those thus brought together, it is certain that many would wait to hear the business of the presbytery, especially if anything interesting was expected. It is more than probable, therefore, that there was a pretty numerous congregation of the Wigtown people present when the accounts of the martyrdom were read in the presbytery;[2] and every man and woman among them, of thirty years of age and upwards, must have known whether these accounts were true or false. On the supposition that they were false, was there no man in the whole community whose moral indignation was aroused? Was there no one to point the finger of scorn against the authors and abettors of so flagrant a falsehood?

(6.) *Mr. Thomas Ker and the Kirk-Session of Wigtown.*

Mr. Thomas Ker, minister of Wigtown from 1701 to 1729, was present in the presbytery on the 27th February 1711, when the Kirk-inner and Penninghame statements were read and sanctioned. It is not possible that he could be ignorant of what was really the fate of the two women. He was ordained minister of Wigtown on the 4th March 1701, not quite sixteen years after the execution is said to have taken place. He must have been in daily communication with his parishioners, who must have been witnesses of it, if it was a fact. And surely an event so extraordinary must have been inquired into

---

[1] The old session-book of Wigtown shows that, in 1723, a number of the people of Wigtown were called before the session because (the meeting of presbytery falling on a New Year's-day) they 'went forth of the town to a public shooting, and ordered the drum to go through the town as the last bell was ringing in order to sermon, which was very displeasing to the presbytery when meeting, being a remarkable contempt of the ordinances of God. Most of the offenders were penitent, and promised better behaviour; but the drummer said, 'he behoved to beat the drum when he was commanded, and appeared to have very little sense of the scandal he had given,' so he was in the meantime suspended from church privileges.

[2] The old session-book of Wigtown shows that the collection at the presbytery meeting on 27th Feb. 1711, was 00:07:08 Scots, which is about half the usual Sabbath collection.

by him; and it cannot be doubted that he had the best information that could be got regarding it, especially after he had been appointed by the Synod of Galloway to bring up to them an account of the sufferings in the bounds of Wigtown Presbytery.

There is, moreover, direct proof, in the old session-book of Wigtown, that this matter was brought under Mr. Ker's notice, in circumstances which could not fail to make him fully acquainted with all the facts of the case. Under date 8th July 1704 it is minuted:—

' *Post preces* sederunt, the minister and all the elders and deacons.' *Inter alia*, ' This day Bailie M'Keand, elder, in Wigtown,[1] addressed this session for the privilege of the sacrament, delaring the grief of his heart that he should have sitten on the seize of these women who were sentenced to die in this place in the year 1685, and that it had been frequently his petition to God for true repentance and forgiveness for that sin. He being removed, and the session enquiring into this affair and the carriage of the said bailie since that time, and being satisfied with his conversation since, and the present evidences of repentance now, they granted him the privilege. He was called in, admonished, and exhorted to deliberation, due tenderness in such solemn address unto God.'

It may be imagined that Bailie M'Keand's ' grief of heart' would not have been so great as it appears to have been, and that he would not have been denied the 'privilege of the sacrament' for nineteen years, had the women, at whose condemnation to death he assisted, not been actually executed. But others may think that, to sentence two women to death for not swearing an oath which their conscience would not allow them to swear, was *in itself* sin enough to call for a very deep repentance. The fact in question cannot be with perfect certainty inferred from Bailie M'Keand's penitence,—though most readers, we think, will be inclined to come to the conclusion that the mere circumstance of his having acted—perhaps very unwillingly—as one of a jury who gave in a verdict followed by a sentence that was never executed, would not, after the lapse of nineteen years, have lain so very heavy on his conscience; and that, if he had been chargeable with no greater crime, he might reasonably enough have complained that *he* should be subjected to discipline for such an offence, when Provost Coltron, who had been somewhat active in fining and imprisoning the Presbyterians, should not merely be unchallenged, but should actually sit as one of his judges.

What deserves especial notice in this session minute, however, is *the men who sat along with Mr. Ker in session when this case was before them,*—men who must have known the whole truth of the case in question, and who must have made Mr. Ker fully acquainted with it. A very strangely constituted man must Mr. Ker have been if he admonished his penitent parishioner without asking what was the actual issue of the case which occasioned his ' grief of heart.'

There is no difficulty in discovering who were the members of Wigtown session at that time; and the minute assures us that they

---

[1] The bailie was not an elder in the church, but is designated ' elder' to distinguish him from Bailie M'Keand, younger, the Christian name of both being John. Bailie M'Keand, younger, was a member of session.

were *all* present. In the minute-book, 13th March 1701, the roll of the session is given; and in a presbytery minute of a visitation of the parish of Wigtown, 4th June 1701, the names of the members of session also appear. Between that date and July 1704, one aged elder, Bailie Soflow, had died, and two elders (both heritors in the parish) and two deacons were ordained on 8th March 1702. Those, therefore, who sat in session with Mr. Ker, when Bailie M'Keand, senior, came before them, were the following:—

1. *William Coltrane* of Drummoral, provost of Wigtown. No one will doubt *his* knowledge of the fact in question. He was in Edinburgh attending Parliament when the case was before the council, and could tell if there was actually a pardon, or what else happened.

2. *John Lafries*, bailie of Wigtown. He is on the roll of the Synod of Galloway, 19th April 1692. He died (between 15th June and 22d July 1711) after the presbytery had received the Kirkinner and Penninghame statements. On the authority of the list of Mr. William Watson, the Episcopal minister of Wigtown, we can state that *John Lafrize* was living at Monkhill, which is close to Wigtown, and commanding a view of the bay, in the end of 1684. That this is the same person, though the name is differently spelled, is proved by the name of his wife, *Elizabeth Ramsay*, which is given in the same list. In the Kirkinner 'ghost' story, which the author of the *Case* has reported, we find that the bailie and the provost were married to sisters. Now, it appears in the list that the provost's wife was *Agnes Ramsay*. The records of the burgh of Wigtown show that John Lafries was in the council in 1687, and was a bailie in 1689.

3. *John M'Keand*, younger, bailie of Wigtown. Ordained before 1701, and died in 1711, after the accounts of the martyrdom were given in to the presbytery. His name is in Mr. Watson's list as residing in Wigtown in the end of 1684, and the burgh records show that he was elected a member of the town council 2d November 1685, John M'Keand, senior, being in the council at the same time.

4. *Thomas Clelland* (tenant in Carslae). On the roll of the synod, 16th October 1694, and his name appears in the session minutes till 1709.

5. *Thomas M'Cleur*. He was an elder before 1701, and his name is in the session minutes till 1715. His name is in Mr. Watson's list as residing in Wigtown in the end of 1684. He was in the town council in 1696.

6. *Patrick M'Kie* of Achleand, ordained 8th March 1702. He was an heritor in the parish of Wigtown, and is designated in Mr. Watson's list as *younger*,—his father, of the same name, being then alive.[1]

---

[1] The records in the sheriff court at Wigtown, under date 19th August 1684, contain the following entry:—' The which day Katherine Lauder, spouse to Patrick M'Kie of Auchlean, confessed that she had withdrawn from the Church these two years bygone, therefore the judge fines the said Auchlean in two hundred and fifty pounds Scots.

        (Signed)   ' DAVID GRAHAM.'

7. *David M'Kie* of Maidland, ordained 8th March 1702. He was an heritor, whose land was close to Wigtown, and whose residence, as appears from the minute-book, was in the burgh. He was a member of session till 1722. He does not appear in Mr. Watson's list, being probably, in 1684, under *twelve* years.

Besides the above elders, there were also present the following deacons:

1. *Michael Shanks*, living in Wigtown, according to Mr. Watson's list, in the end of 1684, and elected a member of town council 2d November 1685; 2. *John Calzie*, in Glenturk, also in Mr. Watson's list; 3. *John Carson*, in the Moss, also in Mr. Watson's list; 4. *John Kevan;* 5. *William Gibson.*

It cannot be doubted that Mr. Ker obtained most reliable testimony as to the actual fate of the 'two women sentenced to die,' when *the affair was inquired into*, in a meeting of twelve Wigtown men,—most of whom, it has been shown, were living there and grown up at the time of the occurrence in question.

In a subsequent minute of the Wigtown session, 23d January 1708, all the members being present,[1] it appears that Mr. Ker laid before the session reasons which he had drawn up for holding a parochial fast, which reasons were approved of and recorded, and the fast appointed to be held. There are seven reasons given at length for observing a fast; and the *second* reason is, that 'the sins of the late unhappy times have not been thoroughly searched out, laid to heart, and mourned over.' Then follows an enumeration of these sins,— 'the sacrificing of the interests of the Lord Jesus Christ and the privileges of His Church unto the lusts and will of men; the establishing of iniquity by law; the apostasy of many unto Prelatical and Erastian courses; the imposing and taking of unlawful oaths, declaration, test, and others of that kind, which were expressly contrary to our reformation and most solemn national engagements; the persecuting, imprisoning, racking, shooting, hanging, *drowning*, beheading, and banishing at pleasure, such as adhered to the truths of God, reformation, and covenants, and refused to prostitute their tender consciences by conformity to the common courses of the times;— though these things be forgotten and buried in oblivion by many, yet they are not forgotten by God, but on the account of these, together with other sins, He is yet pleading a controversy with the land.'

It thus appears that Mr. Ker and the elders of Wigtown included 'drowning' in the list of the sins of the late unhappy times that had still to be laid to heart and mourned over. How could they have done so, had the only persons sentenced to that death never suffered it? Except the two women in question, it is not said that any other was put to death by drowning; so that the minute above quoted may be regarded as a direct assertion of the fact in question, by those who,

---

[1] The session was constituted as above stated, except that Provost Coltron did not now act as an elder; and two other elders had been ordained in 1705—Samuel M'Naught and William M'Caul.

living in Wigtown at the time, had the best means of knowing whether
or not it really took place.

Keeping in mind, then, who were the men with whom Mr. Ker,
minister of Wigtown, was associated in his kirk-session, and what
opportunities he thus had of knowing the true history of Margaret
Lauchlison and Margaret Wilson, it cannot surely be imagined that
he sat in the Presbytery on the 27th February 1711, and heard the
Kirkinner and Penninghame accounts of their sufferings read, and
gave his consent to the transmission of these accounts to Edinburgh,
to be published as history, unless on the supposition that he knew
them to be true. No one who reads the minutes of the Wigtown
Session during the twenty-seven years of Mr. Ker's incumbency, will
believe him to have been either a very wicked or a very foolish man;
but he must have been both, had he, as a member of the Presbytery
of Wigtown, given his concurrence to the publication of a story of
martyrdom, which he must have known to be utterly false.

(7.) *Acquiescence of the Public.*

The proceedings of the two kirk-sessions and of the presbytery
regarding the case in question must have been well known, at least
in the town of Wigtown and throughout the bounds of the presbytery;
and had a false account of the matter been given,—false in the worst
sense, because wilfully so,—there would have been an outcry against
these ministers and elders, some echoes of which would have come
down to our times. Such a scandal would not have remained 'latent'
for a century and a half, then to burst all at once on their great-grand-
children, in the form of a pamphlet of 142 pages, entitled ' *The Case
for the Crown* in re *the Wigtown Martyrs proved to be Myths* versus
*Wodrow and Lord Macaulay, Patrick the Pedler, and Principal Tul-
loch, by Mark Napier, Sheriff of Dumfriesshire.*' There were, perhaps,
few Jacobites in Wigtownshire in those days to raise the cry, but there
was no lack of sinners of other sorts, who would not have been slow
to point the finger of scorn against the rulers of the kirk, could they
have called them *liars*, in return for the too public attention which
they sometimes directed towards less aggravated sins. But it does
not appear that the story of the Wigtown ' suffering' was ever cast in
their teeth; and they seem to have been able, after 1711 as before it,
to pronounce the word ' sufferings' without shame in the presence of
honourable men. The presbytery minutes show that, on the 29th
January 1712, ' Mr. Ker is appointed to consult the sheriff court book
with respect to those sufferings, and apply to Dalreagle[1] for that end.'
Mr. Ker reports (17th May) that the Sheriff-clerk hesitated to grant
the leave asked, 'till he had consulted the Sheriff anent it,' upon
which Mr Ker is again appointed ' to insist for access to consult the
said registers.' On the 2d July, 'the presbytery appoint Messrs.
Seaton (of Glasserton) and William Campbell (of Kirkinner) instantly to repair to the Sheriff (Sir James Agnew), who is in Dal-

[1] Alexander Agnew of Dalreagle, Sheriff-clerk.

reagle's house, and discourse him and Dalreagle anent this affair, and report.'   Messrs. Seaton and Campbell report ' that they went to Sir James Agnew, Sheriff, who allows the presbytery the sight of the said registers, and to get extracts of what may be necessary and useful for them, for clearing the sufferings of the late tymes for religion; and the presbytery appoint Messrs. Seaton, Ker, and William Campbell, to take a convenient tyme betwixt and the next to consult the said registers, and get those things extracted that may be useful.' [1].

It is not easy to imagine men who had been guilty of giving currency to a notoriously false story of a martyrdom that had taken place in Wigtown, going to Sir James Agnew, the Sheriff, to ask leave to search for other cases of suffering in the records of his court; and it is still more difficult to conceive that, on this supposition, he gave them a courteous reception, and trusted them to take excerpts from the records in his keeping.

From the minutes of the Presbytery of Wigtown, 21st January 1719, it appears that all the ministers had subscribed for Wodrow's *History* (then about to be published), except two, who then agreed to subscribe.   This history of the Church of Scotland, compiled by Wodrow chiefly from materials furnished to him by the courts of the church, was published in 1722, and dedicated to the King.   Then, if not before, the story of the Wigtown martyrdom got wide and general circulation.   It was now thirty-seven years after the event, but some who had been actors in the tragedy were still living; [2] and most of the ministers and elders who drew up the two session minutes, and attested them as true, and who were thus the *real authors* of this passage in Wodrow's *History*, still survived.   Mr. Rowan had died before this time; but several of the Penninghame elders who had sanctioned the minute were still living: and Thomas Wilson, now an elder in Penninghame, as has been proved, was living in 1734.   Several of the

---

[1] The brethren thus appointed do not seem to have availed themselves very largely of the liberty allowed to them of making extracts.   On 13th January 1713, they reported that they observed those particulars which the presbytery thought fit to record.   ' 1. That during the time of the late Episcopacy, Sir Andrew Agnew, sheriff-heritabley, was exaucterate of his office, and Claverhouse and his brother put in his place, who received from a great many persons in this shire bonds for money borrowed or received from said Claverhouse, though it is well known that these people never had any business with these persons in the world, which bonds were for fines imposed upon the people for their nonconformity.   2. Authentic documents were seen and read by them of the forfaitures of the estates of Hay of Harriallon, of Alexander Hunter of Culquassen, of Alexander M'Kie of Drumbuie and others, instructing their lands thus forfault (to be) set in tack to tenants by Sir Robert Grier of Lagg; and the said tenants processed and descerned for mails and duties, at the instance of the said Lagg, in the sheriff court.   3. M'Kie of Auchland, his spouse, fined for not keeping the church, though her husband deponed that for much of the tyme she was confined to her house by affliction.   M'Keachie, in Borland, and several others, were fined for nonconformity.   4. Persons debtors to James Softla, merchant, Wigtown; William Thorburn, late provost of Stranraer; William Wilson, merchant there, were descerned to pay the said sheriff several sums of money due to the said persons, as the records in themselves more fully bear.'

[2] Sir Robert Grierson died on 23d December 1733.—*Scots Worthies.*

Kirkinner Session of 1711 were yet alive. Mr. Thomas Ker, minister of Wigtown, lived till 1729 ; and indeed most of the members of the Presbytery of Wigtown, who made themselves responsible for the fact of the Wigtown execution, were still living, to answer for what they had done, when Wodrow's work made that sad story known all over the kingdom. Of the landed proprietors who, being natives of the district, knew the facts of the case, many still survived. Sir James Agnew, the Sheriff, resigned his office to his son in 1723, but lived for many years after that date.[1]

The year 1722 (not the year 1863) was clearly the time to write the *Case for the Crown*, provided the Crown had any case. There were doubtless more Jacobites then than now; and had the history given by Wodrow been false and calumnious, as it is now said to be, it is morally certain that some one would then have proved, when it could easily have been proved, the *negative* in the case of the Wigtown martyrdom. Prior to the publication of Wodrow, it appears that there were some who denied this cruel act of the late Government. Sir George Mackenzie, as has been shown, did so in an *indirect* way, and others after him doubtless did the same ; but no one attempted to clear the Government of this charge by a direct proof. Wodrow refers to such denials, and assigns as the reason for giving this piece of history at greater length, that ' the advocates for the cruelty of this period, and our Jacobites, have the impudence some of them to deny, and others to extenuate, this matter of fact, which can be evinced by many living witnesses.' Here a challenge was openly given to prove the negative, but no one in that age ventured to accept of it. No one then came forward to say, as Mr. Napier now says, ' That is a calum- nious fable from beginning to end,' and to prove that it was a fable by the testimony of living witnesses. Would the adherents of the late Government have allowed such a calumny to rest upon them, if they had been able so easily to wipe it off ? Would they have missed the chance of proving a charge of wilful falsehood against the Church of Scotland, and thus destroying the credibility of the history in all its other details, if they had been able to do their cause so great a service ? No one can believe this. The fact that Wodrow's challenge was un- answered at the time, and that his statement remained uncontradicted for a century and a half, is proof of itself—even were there no other —that the story is true.

5. *Monumental Evidence.*

The only branch of the evidence which still remains to be noticed, is that afforded by the tombstones erected in the churchyard of Wig- town in memory of the drowned women.

Mr. Napier says of the monument raised a few years ago at Wig- town in commemoration of their martyrdom, that it ' like a tall bully lifts the head and lies,' thus entirely misapplying Pope's line on the monument in London. Such a use of Pope's words, in fact, shows

[1] *History of Hereditary Sheriffs*, pp. 522, 529.

that the author of the *Case* is altogether ignorant of their original application. The London Monument, which was erected in 1671–7, to commemorate the Great Fire of London in 1666, bore at first an inscription
saying that the burning was 'begun and carried on by the treachery
and malice of the Popish faction, to carry out their project of extirpat-
ing the Protestant religion.' It was in regard to this statement in the
inscription, therefore, and not in reference to the fact of the fire which
it commemorated, that Pope said it 'lied.' It is easy to understand
how, in writing an inscription for a monument or a tombstone, men's
passions and prejudices may lead them to make statements which,
though they believe them to be true, are not perfectly correct. Our
own times, as well as past ages, have seen examples of this. But it is
one thing to believe that a monumental inscription states incorrectly
the cause of the death of the person buried there, and another to say
that it does not commemorate his death at all. The monument in
London may, and probably did 'lie,' as to the cause it assigned for the
Great Fire—and this, though it gave the opinions of contemporaries.
But this does not disprove the fact of the fire. It bore, and still bears,
irrefragable testimony on this point.

So with the old tombstone to Margaret Wilson,—the story of which
the modern monument merely repeats. It may be that it is in error
in asserting that she was 'murthered for no more crime but not abjuring presbytry, and her not owning prelacy ;' and Mr. Napier may
hold that it incorrectly says that she was 'condem'd by unjust law,'
seeing that he is of opinion that the statute which decreed that women
who insisted on attending field-preaching, and refused to disown on
oath the principles of Renwick's Proclamation, SHOULD BE DROWNED,
was one '*not of barbarous cruelty, but of careful criminal justice*,' and
'*as humane as the condition of the country could possibly admit of*.' Nay,
further, it may be wrong in stating that 'Lagg, Strachan, Winram, and
Grhame,' were all 'actors of this cruel crime.' But even admitting
that the erectors of the monument made violent and incorrect statements in regard to the cause of Margaret Wilson's death, it does not
follow that they were in error as to the *fact* and *time* of her death, any
more than it does, that the London Monument which 'lied' as to the
cause of the fire, commemorates something which never took place.
When, therefore, Mr. Napier asserts that 'whatever the condition of
the old stone or stones, whether in the wall of the church or on the
ground, they can add not one iota of proof in support of the martyrdom, nor detract in the slightest degree from the proof against it ;' and
when he adds that, even if the inscription now on Margaret Wilson's
tombstone did really 'appear in such a work as the *Cloud of Witnesses*, published in 1714,'[1] this 'affords no proof whatever of the
martyrdom,'—he shows clearly that he does not apprehend the nature

[1] Mr. Napier's insinuation (*Case for the Crown*, p. 137), that it is doubtful whether
it was 'actually inscribed on a tombstone at the time of the publication,' hardly merits
serious notice. The supposition that, if it had no real existence, such a statement would
have been made in a work of which, even at that period, three editions appeared in six-

of the proof which such evidence affords.[1]   For if it can be shown that
the monument in Wigtown churchyard was erected during the lifetime of those who were personally cognisant of the events of 1685,
and by those who were either spectators of, or at all events thoroughly
conversant with the fact it commemorates, the truth of the fact itself
—though not necessarily of all the details connected with it—is placed
beyond question ;—at least with those amenable to the ordinary rules
of evidence, though not perhaps in the opinion of one who has avowed,
that if Thomas Wilson 'actually attested the fate of his sister,' he
would merely have 'attested for truth that which is proved to be
false.'

What, then, is the state of the matter in regard to this point ?
The inscription, of which we have given a *facsimile* from a photograph in the frontispiece, is as follows :[2]—

HERE LYES MARGRAT
WILLSON DOUGHTER
TO GILBERT WILLSON
IN GLENVERNOCH
WHO WAS DROUNED
ANNO 1685 AGED 18

LET EARTH AND STONE STILL WITNES BEARE
THEIR LYES A VIRGINE MARTYR HERE.
MURTHER'D FOR OUNING CHRIST SUPREAME,
HEAD OF HIS CHURCH AND NO MORE CRIME.
BUT NOT ABJURING PRESBYTRY.
AND HER NOT OUNING PRELACY
THEY HER CONDEM'D, BY UNJUST LAW ;
OF HEAVEN NOR HELL THEY STOOD NO AW
WITHIN THE SEA TY'D TO A STAKE
SHE SUFFERED FOR CHRIST JESUS SAKE
THE ACTORS OF THIS CRUEL CRIME
WAS LAGG· STRACHAN· WINRAM· AND GRHAME
NEITHER YOUNG YEARES, NOR YET OLD AGE·
COULD STOP THE FURY OF THEER RAGE.

Mr. Napier says, 'We assume that the epitaph to Margaret Wilson,
which appears in the later editions of the *Cloud of Witnesses*, was also
published in the original edition of 1714.   But we have been able to
discover only two copies of that edition, and in both of them the appendix of epitaphs happens to be imperfect.'   We, too, have seen several
copies of the first edition of this work, but none of them contains the
inscription.   At first we thought them imperfect ; but we now doubt
this, and are inclined to think that the first edition did not contain
the Wigtown inscription.   It does not follow, however, that though
not contained in the first edition, it was not in existence when it was

teen years, and which was then universally read in the south and west of Scotland, is
utterly untenable.

[1] On this point reference may be made to Leslie's *Short and Easy Method with the
Deists*.   The fact is, if Mr. Napier's canons of criticism be correct, certain histories of
infinitely greater importance than Wodrow's are endangered.

[2] As the inscription on Margaret Lauchlison's tombstone is not given in the *Cloud
of Witnesses*, and as we have not the same means of determining its date, we have not
referred to it in the argument in the text.   She is, however, evidently enough referred
to in the last two lines of Margaret Wilson's epitaph.   The two tombstones are—judging
from the carving of the letters, the T's and H's and E's being joined in precisely the
same way in both—of the same date, but they are different in size and form, that of
Margaret Lauchlison being a small erect stone, and the other a larger flat one.   This
seems to indicate that they had not been erected by the same parties by public subscrip-
tion, but by relatives or personal friends.

published. Indeed, the way the appendix is introduced, shows that it did not pretend to give a complete list. The notice to the reader says: 'To fill up the vacancy of some pages, 'tis conceived that it will be neither impertinent to the subject, nor unacceptable to the reader, to insert the following EPITAPHS or inscriptions that are on the TOMBS or GRAVESTONES of the martyrs in several churchyards and other places where they ly buried.' This seems to account for the imperfect appearance of the volume,—*the last page being printed down to the very bottom without even space being left for the word* FINIS,—thus showing that the printer had more inscriptions beside him which the 'vacancy' would not contain.[1]

We have not been able to obtain a sight of the second edition of the *Cloud of Witnesses*, but we have been told that the inscription does not appear in it. So far as is at present known, it appeared in print for the first time in the third edition, published in 1730. In this edition, which is in 12mo, the first having been in 4to, a number of additional inscriptions is given, and it is expressly said in the title-page that it is 'amended and enlarged with the testimony of John Richmond, and the inscription upon the gravestone of those who suffered at Magus Muir, with the Inscriptions of several others *omitted in the former Editions*,'—showing that the editor had them beside him previously, but had not inserted them for want of room. The monument to Margaret Wilson must therefore, *at the very latest*, have been erected some time before 1729, that is, within about forty years of the event, though, judging from the antique cutting of the letters, those best qualified to judge place it much earlier in the century.[2] But be the exact date what it may, it is clear that it was erected during the lifetime, and therefore with the sanction of Thomas Ker, who had come to the parish only sixteen years after the event in question, and who had constant personal intercourse for many years with Provost Coltron, Bailie M'Keand, and others who had been personally connected in one way or other with the sentence,—during the lifetime of all the older inhabitants of Wigtown and the neighbourhood, who could not fail to remember the events of the memorable visits of the Commissioners during 'the killing time,'—and, above all, during the lifetime of Thomas Wilson, the brother of the sufferer, who was an elder in the neighbouring parish. Is it possible, then, to conceive any one venturing to commit such an outrage on truth and propriety, as to inscribe on a tombstone in a churchyard visited every Sunday by the whole population of a county town, what they all would have known to be a mere 'fable?'

---

[1] It is worth noticing, that the *last* inscription given in the first edition is that which immediately precedes the one on Margaret Wilson's tombstone in the third and all succeeding editions. Some copies we have seen of the first edition—*e.g.* that in the Advocates' Library—want a leaf of inscriptions which is found in others.

[2] Of course, if it turn out that the inscription was published in the first edition of the *Cloud of Witnesses*, the proof, though the same in *kind*, will be proportionally stronger in *degree*.

The candid reader, who has given his attention to the foregoing proof, will not, it is anticipated, require long time to consider his verdict. Without hesitation, he will say that the women who were condemned at Wigtown in 1685 were actually drowned there; that Wodrow's character as a historian has sustained no damage by the pleadings in the *Case for the Crown*; and that the ministers and elders of the Church of Scotland in Galloway were not guilty of placing on the page of history a story of martyrdom to which the terms 'false and calumnious' can be applied. Wodrow, vindicated on the point on which his credibility has been assailed, will be held to be vindicated as to his other narrations of facts. The people of Scotland will still look upon the tombs of their martyrs with wonted veneration. They will still peruse the annals which record the struggles and sufferings of their fathers in the sacred cause of civil and religious liberty as a faithful page of history, and strive to learn from it the lessons which it teaches.

Those, too, who have taken the negative side of this controversy (which we trust is now ended), will, it is to be hoped, be taught a useful lesson, and will prosecute their researches in the field of history with more candour and charity, and under the guidance of sounder canons of historical evidence. And men generally, we hope, will be instructed by the foregoing pages to have a stronger faith in the recorded events of the past, and not to be easily persuaded, that any statement of fact, credibly vouched and accepted as true at first, which has stood the ordeal to which all history is subjected before it is generally received, and which, after being so tested, has taken and kept its place on the page of history, can after all be really false.

THE END.

MURRAY AND GIBB, EDINBURGH,
PRINTERS TO HER MAJESTY'S STATIONERY OFFICE.

LaVergne, TN USA
18 August 2010
193773LV00004B/26/A